Contents

Sign up to the FREE eBay UK Bulletin

If this book has helped you with your eBay business and you would like to know more, why not sign up for my free weekly newsletter and keep up-to-date with the latest developments for eBay buyers and sellers. You can also send me your feedback and tell me how this book has kick-started your eBay adventure.

Distributed by the publisher of this book – Harriman House – each e-mail contains hints and tips for eBay sellers, news on the latest technical developments on eBay, readers' letters ("Ask Molly") and other essential information. HTML issues are also covered, with explanations of when and how to use additional codes to drive your profits higher. Plus, I check out new ideas regarding sales techniques and provide advice on how to move with the markets.

It's not all work and no play. There are always strange and crazy things happening on eBay and in my "Trader's Tales" section, I share some of the more amusing stories. Like the guy who bought 'half a kilo of Lego' and then was disappointed with the amount! Not to mention the weird and wonderful auctions that take place online – how much would you bid for an 'air guitar' or an 'animatronic rhino'?

You can also keep up-to-date with my own eBay career; I'll share my experiences, both good and bad, with you, so that you can avoid my mistakes and learn from my successes.

To sign up to my free newsletter, please visit:

www.ebaybulletin.co.uk

Best wishes,

Bob (Mollybol)

About the author

After 24 years working for the same company, and many years within the corporate sales division, Bob realised when he hit 40 that it was time for a change.

He began selling on eBay in January 2003, initially by clearing his house of unwanted items, with very little knowledge of computers and no experience of selling via the internet. The first few months were a steep learning curve, but he soon became an established eBay PowerSeller and has sold over 15,000 items to date.

Now aged 42, he has retired from full-time work. Instead, trading under the eBay ID of "Mollybol" he uses eBay to generate an income as and when required.

Bob's first book, 'The eBay Business Handbook', was published in April 2006 and soon became a best seller. Following the success of that book and in response to the many e-mails sent in by readers, Bob began writing 'The eBay UK Bulletin', a weekly e-mail newsletter sent free to thousands of readers. Bob also has his own website at www.ebaybulletin.co.uk where you can catch up with daily life on eBay and follow his eBay career.

Since the publication of his first book, Bob has been invited on to numerous radio shows to share his expert knowledge and inspire others to set up eBay businesses:

"As eBay is now a part of life, we were very privileged to broadcast a programme about it. It's changed people's lives completely – it's a monster that has grown and grown and has made so much money, for so many people. Bob was so enthusiastic on-air and actually taught me a hell of a lot about eBay – and what a great book he has written too."

– Pete Price, Presenter, *Radio City*

For more information and to read the back catalogue of the eBay bulletin – offering tips, advice and real-life stories about the world's most famous online marketplace – sign up today, at: www.ebaybulletin.co.uk

Preface

Buying and selling on eBay is straightforward – most users grasp the fundamentals in under an hour. However, using eBay to its full potential is more challenging. The more you use the site, the more you become aware of its depth, its subtleties, its features and tools that may not at first have been apparent. Even 'veterans' who think they know every wrinkle of the site admit, if pushed, that there is always more they could learn.

I first realised that there was a need for a Q&A book when I reviewed the hundreds of questions sent to me by readers of my weekly bulletin. Looking through the masses of emails and the transcripts of my radio shows, two things struck me:

- Firstly, lots of people ask the same questions. There seem to be certain concepts that stump people every time and no matter how eBay tries to explain them on its website, they continue to baffle.

- Secondly, that some of the questions are quite sophisticated. Many people, it seemed, are comfortable with the basic workings of eBay but get snagged on some of the more esoteric points.

For both types of question, it seemed obvious to me that providing answers in a simple, at-a-glance format would be a useful service.

What you have here, then, is a cross section of questions relating to almost every aspect of eBay and, more importantly, answers which are short, practical, and based on real-life experience; mine, and that of other experienced eBay traders.

Whether you are mainly a buyer or a seller and irrespective of the number or value of trades you do, you should find something in these pages that makes you exclaim "well I never knew that!", "ah, I've always wondered how to do that!" or "now that's an idea!"

Who this book is for

When my children were younger, I would visit their school on parents' day and be told by their teachers that they should ask more questions and not be nervous about raising their hands. Their fear of being "the only person in class who didn't know the answer" was of course unfounded, as most of the rest of the class didn't know either.

This book is, in a way, similar. It is for all those eBay buyers and sellers who have a question, but who have either never got round to asking it or who didn't know who to ask.

I've assumed that the reader already knows the very basics of eBay, but no great knowledge of sales techniques or computers is required. In fact, these are two of the areas which I cover in some depth in the book as I know from my bulletin postbag that many people feel their skills could be improved.

The book also covers more advanced topics for those who are already running an eBay business. Using a fresh, common sense approach, I offer you the benefit of my past and present experiences and apply them to a wide range of scenarios.

The questions and answers in this book cover a huge range of subjects, but if you can't see your question in this selection, please e-mail me directly at mollybol@ebaybulletin.co.uk. If I can help, I will.

What the book covers

This book answers a wide range of questions sent to me by readers of 'The eBay UK Bulletin'. They have been selected to represent the interests and concerns of ordinary eBay users.

The broad categories are: how to sell, how to buy, and how to make a living on eBay, all of which are covered in detail. Fraud on eBay warrants a chapter of its own.

There are of course many ways to tackle similar problems; the answers contained in this book are my opinions based on my personal experiences of being an established PowerSeller.

Having sold a huge assortment of items over the years, including two garden sheds, family cars, more Lego than you can imagine, and even the kitchen sink, I will explain what really happens on eBay, how you can manage your activity on the site to your best advantage, and how things can be improved.

Structure of the book

The 200 questions and answers contained in this book have been grouped together into sixteen chapters, each focusing on a particular area of eBay or trading. The book follows a logical progression from chapter one, which covers the first steps of registering on the site and choosing your ID, through to chapter sixteen, which deals with the dull-but-essential aspects of accounts and tax.

Registration and ID

This chapter covers the issues and concerns raised by those new to eBay:

- Setting up an eBay account for the first time; what name to choose and how best to begin your eBay experience.

- Choosing a 'hackproof' password and making it as secure as possible.

- The information you will need to enter online and why it is required.

- The practical aspects of having separate buying and selling accounts on eBay.

Buying issues

Everybody loves a bargain, but finding that needle in the haystack takes more than luck. This chapter deals with some of the pitfalls associated with buying on eBay and also some great ways to bag a bargain.

- The buying process is quite straightforward most of the time; with just a little more research and planning it will become very rewarding. A better understanding of how the bidding process works will improve your chances of success.

- Searching for that elusive deal is much easier if you understand how eBay's systems work, and the facilities that are available. Something that appears to be a bargain isn't always what it seems. This chapter will help you through those first tentative purchases.

- Advice and guidance on the postage and packing details to look out for. Check out your seller and take into account all the costs before making the decision to buy.

- Consider how you will pay for the item, and what represents the best value when buying. Payment protection is an important value added service and should be uppermost in your buying criteria.

Deciding what to sell

This chapter introduces the selling process and highlights some of the issues that regularly crop up. Learn from other sellers' experiences and sell your items in a more structured way.

- Understand the selling process better and how the choices you make impact on your auction results. The best time and method of selling will vary from product to product, but there are some key principles that apply to every trade.

- Ensure you get the maximum price for your item through great auction design. Getting your auction seen by as many buyers as possible is critical; there are a few tricks of the trade to help ensure visibility.

- What to sell and when are key questions for any eBay seller. Take a fresh look at the possibilities and understand more about what will and won't sell well.

Sourcing products to sell

If there is one question that I am asked more than any other, it is "where do you get your stock?" This is perhaps the hardest aspect of an eBay business, but don't despair as there are many ideas covered in this chapter.

- Wholesalers and drop shippers might be the obvious choice, but how exactly do you find one and what can you expect when you place that first order.

- Consider using eBay and other online sites as a source of stock. Learn how to find the bargain that others have missed and resell it at a healthy profit.

- How about selling other people's items on commission? It is not as complicated as it may seem.

Listing items for sale

Chapter 5 takes a closer look at the processes and choices to be made when actually listing an item on eBay. Get this right and you will soon reap the rewards and stand out from the competition.

- What is the best duration and end time for an auction? Is Sunday evening still the optimum time?

- Are the paid-for listing upgrades worth the money? Opinions vary greatly as to the true value of these enhancements; there is after all no point in spending money for no return.

- When you finally secure your buyer, it is in your interest to keep their attention and keep them spending with you. There are a number of tricks of the trade that do the job; they certainly work for me.

Mechanics of the sale

This chapter looks at the day-to-day activities surrounding eBay, the nuts and bolts of a robust business. Although you can never plan for every eventuality, there are many things that can be done to make life just that little bit easier.

- Consider the questions you are likely to be asked and how best to manage these enquiries when sales levels increase.

- This chapter takes a new look at some of the events, both good and bad, which make trading on eBay so eventful.

Postage and delivery

The end of your auction signals the beginning of the despatch phase; not the most enjoyable aspect of the process. However with a little planning and a new approach, it is possible to reduce the tedium of the task.

- Consider what a fair postage charge is. The amount you would be happy to pay is the amount you should charge. Charging for packing materials is fine but be wary about levying too high a 'handling charge'.

- How quickly you dispatch items will help decide your feedback rating. Once a buyer has paid for their item, they want it immediately.

- This section will also expand on the delivery options available; how buyers can reduce postage costs and receive the item just as quickly. First class or second, airmail or surface, parcel or packet; it's all here.

Packing

Hand in hand with the previous chapter, next we take a look at the practical aspects of preparing your item for shipment. This for me is by far the most boring element of the job, but it has to be done and done to a high standard every time.

- What to consider when packing your item that will help achieve a better sale price; reducing your p&p costs will make you more competitive.

- The many options regarding packing materials and where to find them. From recycled boxes to rolls of bubble wrap, ensure that your packing is fit for purpose.

- How do you bubble wrap a sofa? Slowly. Strike the right balance between time and materials; learn from the mistakes of others. Pack and be happy.

When transactions go wrong

It's not all plain sailing, nobody ever said it would be; things do go wrong on eBay just as they can in any transaction. Buying and selling both have their own potential problems, but knowing how to handle them might just give you an edge (and save your sanity).

The internet takes away one valuable thing – the ability to hold a conversation with someone whilst looking them in the eye. Good communication is therefore key for both buyers and sellers.

- The secret to a successful trade is to keep talking; when things go quiet both parties fear the worst. There are some easy ways to facilitate this process.

- Let's talk e-mails; when to send them, which ones and how many. There are automated services to make this easier within the eBay system.

- Problems can, almost always, be resolved and it helps to understand the eBay systems that are available during these times.

Feedback

Feedback is perhaps the best and worst aspect of eBay; it is vital as an aid to judging the track record of a seller, but due to the protective nature of one's feedback score, true feelings are not always accurately reflected.

- When to leave feedback and who should leave it first are questions open to much debate, and a good variety of thoughts are to be found here.

- Building a good track record in the early days is vitally important for a seller, but the buying and selling of feedback is strictly forbidden.

- Questions are great, they mean that somebody is interested and might buy your item. Save time and hassle by getting your listings and answers right first time.

- Would you sue a non-payer? There are other ways to resolve problems and minimise the financial impact.

Payment

Receiving payment is a fundamental part of the process and is what makes it all worthwhile.

- What payments methods will you accept and how will your choice affect the likelihood of a bid? Should you accept money from overseas buyers and, if so, by what methods? What is the credit risk associated to each payment method? Find the answers to these and other questions in this chapter.

Fees, duties and charges

eBay's charging structure can be confusing as it is fairly complex. This chapter takes a look at the trading costs involved; some of them are not quite as obvious as you might expect.

- Buying from an overseas eBay site may land you with a hefty import tax bill, turning your bargain purchase into an expensive purchase. Don't get caught out.

- If you don't pay your eBay fees, they will remove you from the site, but if you are entitled to a refund, ensure you understand the process to get your cash back. How and when this might apply is covered here.

- By far the most interesting aspect of 'fees, duties and charges' is knowing how to reduce them legitimately. This is a topic close to my heart and this chapter draws on my personal experience.

Scams

The title of this chapter says it all: how to recognise and avoid potential fraud associated with eBay trading. This comes in many guises so you have to be on your guard all the time.

- The modern day highwaymen operate on the internet. Crooks see eBay as a hunting ground and will try every trick in the book to defraud you. Expect to be bombarded with e-mails asking for your account details. Treat every seller as a potential fraudster, and always be on your guard.

- Was it really lost in the post? How can you protect yourself from unscrupulous buyers? What protection is available for sellers and what steps must you take to get it?

- You can fall foul of corrupt buyers even if your item does arrive; the 'receive and switch' scam is alive and kicking and you may not even realise you have been conned. Find out how to defend yourself.

- It's not just buyers of course; sellers can be crooked as well. *Caveat emptor* (buyer beware) applies and the buyer must be confident in trading with the seller before parting with any hard-earned money.

- Fakes, fakes, fakes – they are everywhere. How to spot them and what to do next.

Trading for a living

If you are thinking of a career change then I would offer this advice; start small. eBay is a great place to work, and can afford you the freedom to choose your own pace of life, but it can also be fickle. Try it out for size first and make sure it's definitely for you before you tell your boss what you really think of your job.

- This chapter uncovers the secrets of increased selling success; what drives your final prices and profit higher.

- Marketing is a key activity for any business, and eBay is no exception. Reach more customers and watch the money roll in.

- When to sell can be just as important; umbrella sales are slow in the summer and sunglasses are less popular during winter months. Seasonal selling is a fact of life, so learn how to even out the peaks and troughs.

- Increase your auction's success rates, upgrade your auction design and learn more about your customers buying habits.

- Manage your customers' expectations through better use of the eBay tools and features. Enhanced visibility will increase traffic to your listing, but can also reduce your margins. Which features offer value for money?

Technology

Such is the pace of change these days that many find the prospect of internet trading too daunting. There are some technical requirements for trading on eBay; thankfully they are not too onerous.

- How does the 'internet virgin' get started? What do I need to keep my system free from infection? It is never too late to start; my father-in-law is still trading well into his 70s, although I do help out with the HTML from time to time.

Accounts and tax

Keeping on top of the paperwork in any business is a demanding task, and eBay is no different. This last section of the book looks at the boring, but important, aspects of the job:

- Is tax an issue? Should I be charging VAT? Learn what records you need to keep and how you need to keep them.

- Which rules and regulations are likely to trip you up? Read about other traders' experiences and the solutions they have found to the most common problems.

- The dreaded accounts, the bane of all self-employed traders. Keep up to date with the paperwork and the future will be bright.

- At each stage of the book, references are made to my own experiences of selling on eBay, highlighting the pitfalls I've discovered along the way and some of the more interesting ways to make both buying and selling both enjoyable and very rewarding.

Introduction

The doors of the tube slide open, it's jammed full. Those on the platform look at those on the train, who return their gaze; nobody gets off, nobody gets on, the doors close and the train moves off. The station is hot and dirty, crowded with business suits and briefcases; nobody ever smiles.

It was before 8 in the morning and I'm on a tube station at Liverpool Street on my way to a meeting somewhere in London. A typical weekday morning. There must be more to life than this.

It seems a long time ago now, but it was in fact only a little over two years ago that I left the corporate world I had known for 24 years and decided to try my hand at a new life.

As an Account Manager for BT, my job was to grow revenues and profit by putting together multi-million pound deals for major 'blue-chip' companies.

Deciding to leave work and opt for a more relaxed pace of life was the easy bit; finding the money to actually live was another thing altogether. I still had all of the normal responsibilities: a house to run, three children and two useless dogs to support. I needed money.

I have always been successful in sales, but a salesman who doesn't like traffic jams or tube trains has limited prospects and anyway I didn't want to work for somebody else anymore.

Trading online seemed the obvious solution: no commuting; a coffee break whenever I felt like it; and no boss. The attractions were obvious and I began to wonder whether buying and selling items on eBay might provide an alternative. There were lots of articles appearing in the press about how people were running eBay businesses from home, but I had no idea whether the stories were either true or realistic. I had used the site to sell the usual unwanted DVDs and kid's toys, even the garden shed, but that level of activity was hardly enough to give me a livelihood. If I was really going to make a living out of eBay, I'd have to come up with something other than unwanted clutter to sell, a product where I could get consistent supplies, attract plenty of buyers, and make high margins.

On the plus side, I had already established a good feedback score, which meant that potential buyers should be willing to trade with me. I knew that the main obstacle to setting up an eBay business is that customers cannot see the actual goods and have to trust the vendor to actually deliver. They will only do this if they see evidence of a good track record, and on this score I was fine.

Creating the right online environment was also a challenge; my experience up to this point had been purely traditional sales, usually face-to-face, where I could explain the product verbally and with the help of printed brochures. That obviously wouldn't be possible on eBay. Instead I'd have to learn new skills: how to attract people to look at my products, how to ensure that it came up on eBay's search engine, how to write good copy describing it, and how to create the right 'look and feel'. Selling on eBay is completely different. I had picked up a reasonable knowledge of HTML – the coding that decides how things look on a wed page – along the way, so knew I could make a half decent attempt at the aesthetics of an online store.

But what to actually sell, where to get stock and what exactly is drop shipping? If I didn't come up with the answers, my eBay career would be short-lived.

So there I was; aged 40, 3 kids, a house, 2 dogs and bills to pay. I had a half-baked idea about using eBay as a sales channel, but nothing to sell. I had just given back the keys to my company car, handed over my mobile phone, computer, free phone lines, expense account, final salary pension scheme, rather useful salary and huge bonus. And I couldn't have been happier.

Now, two years on, my eBay business has grown to such an extent that a move to larger premises is a possibility; I still have to decide if I want to work that hard. My daily commute is an 8-yard walk, the dogs are still completely useless, but the coffee tastes better somehow.

Chapter 1

Registration And ID

Introduction

In my opinion the most important thing to do when considering buying or selling on eBay for the first time is to put the coffee on and settle down in a comfy chair.

In the early days it's all about understanding how the system works and doing your research. Before you make your first purchase you need to know what to look for in a seller and how to double check that the item really is a bargain. Before selling for the first time, you need to know what demand there is likely to be for your item, the price it is likely to fetch, and how to present it on eBay.

This chapter looks at these basics. Whether it is the user name you select or the best time of day to sell, somebody will have asked a question about it.

What factors should I consider when choosing an ID?

As a seller your eBay ID should be something that is both easy to read and remember. Mollybol, my primary trading ID, doesn't actually mean anything, but it reads like a real word and is phonetically simple. One criticism of it might be that it does not actually tell browsers what I specialise in. If you intend to specialise in a certain type of product, it can be good to choose a name which reflects that. "DVDseller" would be great if you sold DVDs, for example. Most of the best names have already been taken so you may need to spend a little time selecting the right one.

If you already have an ID, but think that it could be improved, it makes sense to switch to a better one now rather than six months down the line when you have a hundred sales under your belt. Your ID is like a brand: choosing a good one, and sticking with it, will encourage recognition and loyalty among your target buyers. Avoid numbers, underscores and random letters as these make your name harder to remember.

As a buyer I don't think your eBay ID is of great significance; your ability to pay quickly is far more crucial to sellers. When you are selling however, I am convinced that having an appropriate trading name makes a great deal of difference. Whether you decide to change your existing name or create a new one, these are my top five tips:

1. Keep it short

   Make your ID easy for bidders to type; don't make them re-write *War and Peace* just to find you.

2. Only use letters

   Avoid using numbers in your name. Letters are easier to remember.

3. Spell out a word

   Make your name something that can be pronounced. A jumble of letters just won't be remembered.

4. Avoid current trends

   Choose a name that won't date, avoid topical films and other subjects that won't mean as much in a few years time.

5. Make it relevant

   If at all possible choose an ID that reflects in some way the kind of thing you intend to sell; you may have to think long and hard as all the good ones are long gone.

How do I go about creating a selling account on eBay?

The process to create a selling account is very straightforward.

1. If you already have an account as a buyer, simply upgrade via your 'My eBay' section.

2. If you are starting from scratch, go to the eBay home page and click on 'Register'.

Private Registration: Enter Information   Help

1 Enter Information   2. Choose User ID & Password   3. Check Your Email

Register now to bid, buy or sell on any eBay site. It's easy and free! Already Registered?

	Your privacy is important to us
Account Type	We do not sell or rent your personal information to third parties for their marketing purposes without your explicit consent.
Private Account	
Change to Business Account	
Business sellers should register with a business account. Learn more about business registration.	To learn more, see eBay's privacy policy.

First name   Last name

Street address

Town / City

County   Post code   Country
-- Select County --   United Kingdom

Primary telephone   Secondary telephone (Optional)
(   )   (   )

Example: (020) 12345678 Needed if there are questions about your account

Date of Birth
--Day--   --Month--   --Year-

You must be at least 18 years old to use eBay

Important: A working email address is required to complete registration.

Email address

Examples: myname@aol.com or myname@yahoo.com

Re-enter email address

eBay's User Agreement and Privacy Policy
In order to use eBay, you must first read and agree to eBay's User Agreement. These are the terms and conditions that apply to your use of eBay. eBay's User Agreement can be viewed and printed by clicking here.

You should also read eBay's Privacy Policy to learn about the ways in which we use and protect your personal information. The Privacy Policy can be viewed and printed by clicking here.

By checking the boxes below, I confirm the following:
☐ I have read and accept the User Agreement and I have read the Privacy Policy.
☐ I agree to receive communications from eBay and understand that I can change my notification preferences at any time in My eBay.
☐ I must be an adult (18 years old) to trade on eBay and I certify that I am an adult and can enter into this Agreement.

The instructions are easy to follow. You will need to enter your personal contact details, an email address and so on. eBay will initially create an account for you as a buyer, which you can then upgrade to a seller's account.

You will be asked for either a credit card number or your bank account details, or possibly both. This is to ensure that eBay can collect their fees when you create your first auction, and you will only have to enter this information once.

There are no upfront charges and you will not need to deposit any money with eBay. If you do begin to sell, you can monitor your account status and track how much you owe eBay in fees. To do this, click on the 'Seller account' link on your 'My eBay' page at any time.

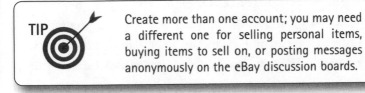

TIP Create more than one account; you may need a different one for selling personal items, buying items to sell on, or posting messages anonymously on the eBay discussion boards.

How can I make my password "hackproof"?

In this age of account hackers, it is surprising just how many eBay users have short, simple, insecure passwords. The eBay password page will helpfully indicate how secure you have made yours as you enter it into the system.

These are my recommendations for a secure password:

1. Ensure your password is longer than 4 characters in length. There are a number of programs available commercially that can instantly hack a password of 4 characters or less (not that I own one I might add!) eBay recommend using at least 6 characters.

2. Use a mixture of upper and lower case letters. This is a feature of the PayPal password security system, but for some reason eBay treats upper and lower case as the same. Adding an upper case letter adds to the complexity, but is not enough on its own.

3. Include numbers and ASCII characters – basically anything that appears on your keyboard such as, !"£$%^&*()>?:@{}. Add a couple of these along with a number or two and the time taken to crack your password will be significantly increased.

4. Use a word that doesn't exist. Have you heard of a "dictionary" attack? Some password hacking programs run through every word in the dictionary until they find your password. The more logical the word, the easier it is to find it. Even joining two words together doesn't slow them down much.

So, an ideal password is one that is a mixture of upper and lower case, is longer than 4 characters, includes numbers and ASCII characters, and is not a real word – that should be easy to remember.

> I have so many passwords now that I have written them all down and keep them with my spare door and car keys in a secret location – you can never be too careful!

Why are there so many places to enter my address details?

It does seem a little strange, but eBay need up to three sets of address details, each of which is likely to be the exactly same. Remember to change the address details if you ever move. I imagine every seller on eBay has sent at least one parcel to an old address because it was not updated.

The address details you need to enter are:

- Registration address: Your main contact address.

- Payment address: Your address where you receive payments. This is very important!

- Primary postage address: Your main postage address for purchases.

You can enter or edit your address details by accessing the 'Addresses' section of your 'My eBay' page.

What advantages are there in registering as a business seller?

On the face of it, registering as a business seller does not have any tangible benefits. There are no favourable terms and no preferential treatment available. In fact a business seller has additional obligations, under UK consumer law (the Distance Selling Regulations 2000), to buyers that personal sellers do not have to worry about.

You do have to be registered as a business seller in order to use 'eBay Express' to sell new products, so this may be reason enough for you.

Harder to determine is the buyer's attitude towards a business seller; maybe they believe that they will get a better service from a professional seller. Many full time traders still operate under the personal banner, so declaring your business interests should give out the message that you are a legitimate trader with nothing to hide.

Business sellers may have completed more trades than other eBay members, which should help assure potential buyers that they are in safe hands.

Business seller status also suggests that you are likely to have informed HMR&C of your trading activities. If you have done this, but chosen not to register as a business seller, somebody may report you anyway, which might cause an inconvenience.

> It still makes me smile when I see a seller with a huge feedback who is selling many identical items but still registered as a private seller. Although this does not really mean anything, I do wonder if they might be pushing their luck just a little too far.

I had to provide my direct debit information. Will eBay charge me for using the site?

It depends what you do on eBay, as you will only be charged by them if you sell an item. Unlike most traditional auctions, there is not a 'buyer's premium' to pay if you win an auction.

If you sell an item you will be billed once a month and if you have elected to pay by direct debit, they will take the money directly from your account.

If you do not sell anything, then eBay will not take any money from your account.

TIP Pay your eBay fees with a credit card that offers reward points and then jet off to the sun. But make sure you don't get into debt!

Will a separate selling account for personal items make my admin any easier?

I would opt for more than one selling ID, particularly a separate one for any private selling you may wish to do as it makes life a lot easier. Depending on what it is you sell, it might make sense to have an account for each specific area of business in which you operate. It may also be the case that having used items alongside new goods might give some buyers the wrong impression of your business.

On the subject of making admin easier, the same idea could also be applied to bank accounts– one account for business number one, another for business two, etc. You can only link one PayPal account to one bank account, which is a bit of a pain, but does provide added security.

TIP Ensure your business PayPal accounts are 'verified'. This will give your buyers added protection and more confidence to trade with you.

I have a completely separate set up for selling my personal items, with a different PayPal account and bank details.

Is it worth registering as a seller on eBay Express?

eBay Express is another route to market for sellers of new items, and is ideally suited to buyers who want to shop quickly and with trusted sellers.

There are some strict criteria which must be followed and the site is only accessible for traders registered as business sellers.

At the time of writing, the number of categories available on eBay Express is quite small; if your category is not there, you cannot list your item. If eBay increase the number of available categories, then it is likely to become increasingly popular with sellers.

To sell on eBay Express, you need to:

1. Be a UK registered seller.

2. Be registered as an eBay business seller.

3. Hold a PayPal Business or Premier account.

4. Complete the PayPal 'Recommended Steps for Merchants' form.

Full details of how to register for eBay Express can be found at:

http://pages.express.ebay.co.uk/service/about/selling.html

What is bank funding on PayPal?

You can opt to have your PayPal payments funded from your bank account; this then becomes your default payment option, allowing you to make payments to a seller using an instant bank transfer.

If there is not enough money in your account to meet the level of payment required, your debit or credit card is used automatically as a back-up funding method.

Only you can request that a payment be made from your bank account. PayPal will never seek to debit funds from your bank account without your authority.

A seller would see this type of payment as an 'echeque'. This could cause them to delay shipment until the payment clears and that could be up to three weeks.

What status do I need to be to become an eBay seller?

The good news is that you don't need a certain level of status to become a seller – the great thing about eBay is that almost anybody can register and start selling.

However, certain aspects of selling do require a minimum feedback score (using the 'Buy it now' (BIN) instant purchase option, for example), and you will need to register a valid card (credit or debit) to verify your account.

To become a seller you'll need to:

Verify your identity

You will need to provide a credit or debit card to create a seller's account; alternatively you can verify your identity by phone. In some cases, you'll also need to provide your bank account information.

If you verify your identity by phone you can start selling on eBay immediately. You will need to enter your landline telephone number and then answer an automated call from eBay. Enter the 4 digit number that will be given to you and continue the registration process.

Select your preferred method of paying seller fees

You can pay your seller fees using any of the following payment methods:

1. PayPal (monthly and one-time payments)

2. Direct debit from your bank account (monthly and one-time payments)

3. Credit card (monthly and one-time payments)

4. Cheque or postal order

Offer PayPal or a merchant account credit card as a payment method

Sellers who registered after 17th January 2007 are required to offer either PayPal or a merchant account credit card as an accepted payment method for their items.

Chapter 2

Buying Issues

Introduction

Everybody loves a bargain and buying on eBay can be a great way to satisfy that urge; just be cautious. Remember the golden rule: If it sounds too good to be true, it probably is. It's always worth taking a step back and assessing whether that vintage avocado bathroom suite is really worth the price you are bidding for it.

This section of the book takes a look at a few of the situations you may find yourself in when you buy on eBay. There are lots of tips along the way too.

Excess postage charges are one of the biggest problems buyers have to contend with; something that is made even worse when you don't know what the postage will actually be before you place your bid. You may find that you can buy the aforesaid bathroom suite for a few quid, but what seemed like a bargain at the time may turn out to be anything but if the seller charges you hundreds of pounds to deliver it.

Almost anything can be bought on eBay for almost any price, making research a key aspect of the process. Use the search engines and compare prices; check out the seller and confirm the postage before bidding. Follow the basic lessons in this chapter and all should be well.

What do you consider to be the key points when buying on eBay?

Making your first purchase on eBay can be a little daunting; there are so many stories about buyers being conned out of their money that it's bound to go wrong, isn't it? Well, for some it does and these examples frequently hit the press. However, many thousands of trades are completed every day without problems.

Whenever you put your hand in your pocket, be slightly wary and do some checking before you buy. These are my top five tips for a safer purchase:

1. Check the seller's feedback score: The higher the number after the seller's name, the more trades they have completed. It's their track record of reliability.

2. Read the feedback comments: What buyers write about the seller will give a great insight into the service you are likely to receive.

3. Check that the item for sale is within the range normally sold: Be cautious if the seller usually has small value auctions, but is now offering a number of items with a significantly higher value.

4. Use PayPal wherever possible as it's free for buyers: Check the level of "buyer protection" offered (top right of the listing page), and if the seller is verified then they are being underwritten by PayPal.

5. A genuine X-Box 360 for £50.00! If it sounds too good to be true, it probably is. Exercise the same levels of caution and common sense on eBay as you would when buying anywhere else.

I am unsure exactly what to sell on eBay, how should I start?

Deciding what to sell on eBay may be immediately obvious to you if you already have a hobby that could produce an income. You may already have access to a stock of items and just need a way to sell them.

It is certainly worth checking what sells in your area of interest. This will not only provide you with an insight into the viability of the products you are considering, but also show you the techniques used by similar sellers.

Start with an easy item

Understanding the sales process is as important as having the right items to sell. Start by selling something that is easy to describe and post; it does not have to be of high value. This will allow you to gain experience of the eBay systems and highlight some improvements that you could make second time around. Once you have mastered the process of selling on eBay, almost anything can be sold in much the same way.

Why do I always seem to be outbid as soon as I place my bid?

I remember my first experience of bidding. I wondered how somebody could top my bid so quickly after I had placed it; they must be glued to the screen watching for any changes.

Of course it is not actually like that, eBay uses a proxy bidding system. It is the same as leaving your maximum bid with a traditional auctioneer. The eBay system places a bid on your behalf and if that bid is beaten, it will bid again but only up to your maximum amount. The increments of these bids are pre-determined by eBay and dictated by the current high bid.

For example, if your maximum bid was £4.00, you could be beaten by as little as 20p if the winner bid either £4.20 or £5.00. eBay will bid on their behalf such that they win by the smallest amount allowable.

The final moments of an auction tend to see an increase in bidding activity. This is because some buyers watch an auction and only place their bid towards the very end. Their thinking is that if they bid earlier, they will get into a battle with other bidders and drive the price higher. By entering the race in the last minute (or last few seconds) they hope to snatch victory by bidding the highest price and not allowing anyone else time to respond. Automated programmes (sniping software) can also be used to place your bid (up to your maximum amount) in the final seconds of the auction. This software means you don't even need to be at a computer when the auction is ending. However or whenever the bids are placed, it will always be the person who placed the highest bid within the allotted time that wins the item.

In the event of two identical bids being placed, the earliest bid wins.

What do I do if the seller won't accept my payment?

The most likely reason is that bidding did not get as high as they had hoped and they just don't want to complete the trade. This can be very frustrating for a buyer and as you would expect there is an eBay form that should help. The "Non-selling seller policy" governs seller performance, and full details can be found at:

http://pages.ebay.co.uk/help/policies/seller-non-performance.html

The first thing to do is report the seller via this link. Send eBay as much information as possible, including copies of e-mails which can be copied into the form. Although it is very hard to make a seller actually complete the trade, eBay might just apply enough pressure.

> I find it hard enough to make the sale in the first place, never mind not taking the money.

If I place too high a bid by mistake, what can I do?

You can usually retract your bid and enter the amount again. I say usually as there is a time limit which restricts this activity towards the end of the auction duration.

Check the rules on bid retraction at:

http://pages.ebay.co.uk/help/buy/bid-retract.html

If there are more than 12 hours remaining, retract your bid and re-enter a new amount. If there are less than 12 hours to go, contact the seller who is able to cancel bids right up until the auction closes. If the auction ends and you have not managed to retract or cancel your bid, you will be at the mercy of the seller; contact them as soon as possible and grovel profusely – this always works with me.

Why would a seller cancel my bid for no apparent reason?

There are several reasons why a seller might cancel your bid; it could be that they perceive a problem with you, or they have a problem with the item.

If the item is no longer for sale, perhaps it has been sold at a fixed price or removed for any number of reasons, then the seller will cancel all bids that had been placed on it. If the item is still on eBay and it appears that yours in the only bid to have been removed, I would suggest e-mailing the seller using the 'Ask seller a question' facility and enquire as to why your bid was removed.

Many sellers stipulate a minimum feedback requirement for bidders; it may be that you do not have a high enough feedback rating. Sellers tend to apply this rule because it is often new eBay members that cause problems post sale and do not complete the trade.

How can I be sure that an item is not a fake?

Did you know that you can get fake Lego? It is not very good and is easily spotted, but it does show that everything can be copied.

Fakes and copies are not allowed to be sold on eBay. Some of them are so bad, i.e. films copied onto blank DVDs with no plastic boxes, that they are easily identified and can be removed from the site. Watch out for the seller who will ship the item without a box in order to cut down on p&p – exactly how much does a DVD case weigh?

Big brand names are the most likely to be copied and those with a high ticket price more so. Watches and jewellery are common targets for copies; be particularly wary of designer items that are being shipped from foreign shores.

If you are in any doubt about the authenticity of an item, contact the seller and ask for more details or some close up pictures of any labels and accompanying paperwork. There is an option to make eBay aware of any suspect items, and a 'Report this item' link is provided at the bottom of each listing page.

> I don't own a watch, so spotting the genuine article would be impossible for me therefore I simply won't be buying one!

Are sellers allowed to offer bonus items with the main item they are selling?

Yes, it's quite a nice idea for a sales promotion, and I have used it in the past. There is just one extra thing that needs to be included in the listing and that is the actual price at which the bonus kicks in. If it is a "Dutch auction" also known as a "multiple auction listing" and the final price reaches the bonus level, all winners must be awarded the bonus item.

Giveaway items that are not of significant value in relation to the actual item cannot be mentioned in the title. Buyers may be misled when searching. In the case of a computer game given away with a console, it might be ok to mention this in the title as it probably has a significant value of its own.

> **TIP** If you do offer a bonus item, consider the impact on postage costs – bonus items are likely to make the parcel weigh more.

I am thinking of buying a car on eBay, but how do I know that it is not a 'write-off'?

Buying a car can be a problem using the more traditional methods, but when buying one from eBay, it is likely that you will not even have seen it. The main concern will often be "is the car stolen?" To put the buyer's mind at rest and to stimulate more sales, eBay offer the option to purchase a Vehicle Status Report, currently at a cost of £6.99.

The report will indicate whether the car:

- Is an insurance write-off.

- Has an outstanding loan on it.

- Has been reported as stolen.

- Has any mileage inconsistencies recorded on the National Mileage Register (NMR).

Although this report cannot guarantee that all is well with the vehicle, it is a good start and, in my opinion, £6.99 well spent.

You can view a sample report here:

www.vehiclestatusreport.co.uk/check/sampleResults.do

> I have bought one car so far and that went without a hitch, so from my personal experience it is worth considering. I have also sold two cars on eBay, both of which exceeded my expectations on price.

Only twice have I sent an item before receiving payment, on both occasions to Germany. I used to have COD listed as a payment option. In Germany it is quite usual for the receiver of a parcel to pay the postal worker who delivers, they in turn redirect the money to the sender. I had no awareness of this and of course could not include the appropriate paperwork; I am still at a bit of a loss as to who would trade in this way. All was well in both cases – once the buyers realised that I didn't understand, but had sent the items in good faith, both sent the funds to me. However, this is *not* something I would recommend and I no longer have COD as a payment option.

If I'm worried about a seller, can I ask him to send the item before I pay for it?

Well, you could try this approach, but be prepared for a short and succinct reply. If I were a seller making my first tentative sale on eBay, I would be reluctant to send my item prior to being paid, even to somebody with a high feedback rating.

There would certainly be no harm in sending an e-mail asking a few further questions about the item. You may be able to judge further from the answers received. If the seller accepts PayPal, I would use this as the payment method and may even be tempted to pay extra and have it posted by special delivery, especially if it is of reasonable value.

Is there a way to search for items being sold near to where I live?

Yes, it is very easy and a great way to look for larger items such as cars, kitchens or a Gulf-stream jet! The 'Advanced Search' facility will take care of this extra criterion. Firstly, click on the Advanced Search link at the top right of any eBay screen; you will need to be logged into the site to do this. In the list of search options, click the box labelled 'Items near me', enter your postcode and the distance you are prepared to travel.

Using this search, I found 14 sellers of sheds within 25 miles of Mollybol HQ and even one seller offering a "chicken run" for sale. Not quite sure why I searched for that, stuck for gift ideas at Christmas I guess!

How do I know that I can trust the seller?

The simple answer is that you can never be 100% sure – even PowerSellers with huge feedback scores sometimes go bad – but there are some precautions that you can take which will reduce the likelihood of any problems. Be extra careful if the seller states in big letters 'SOLD AS SEEN' or 'NO REFUNDS', something is bound to be wrong with the item.

These are my top five tips:

1. Check out the seller's feedback score *and* comments.

2. Does the seller have Payment Protection?

3. What else are they selling?

4. Check the seller's terms and conditions.

5. Check the p&p costs and their Ts & Cs.

If these elements don't look right, move on to another seller.

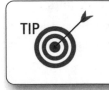

TIP Be aware that if you deal with a seller who won't accept PayPal, you are accepting all the risk to save them money on fees!

Why should I have a separate eBay ID for buying items?

It's not essential to opt for a separate eBay ID for purchases, but it can make life a bit simpler. Having more than one ID won't cost any more but you will need a different e-mail address. The main reasons for considering a separate buying ID are:

• Concealing the price you paid

   If you buy from eBay and resell for a profit, it might become awkward if you use the same ID. The original seller, for one, might not be too impressed.

- Freedom to express your views

  If the purchase goes wrong and you decide to leave negative feedback, any retaliatory comments will not be logged against your main selling ID.

- Keeping competitors in the dark

  The use of a different buying ID will not provide your competitors with any information as to the source of your stock.

The seller does not have the item in stock, but has taken my money. What should I do?

This is a classic case of poor inventory management on behalf of the seller. High volume sellers with many product lines cannot always see exactly how many items they have left, and have to rely on an inventory management system to track stock for them. Unfortunately this process sometimes goes wrong.

It is likely that the problem was not apparent until somebody went to pick the item ready for dispatch, by which time they would, of course, have taken your money.

If the seller has a good feedback record and is still active on eBay, there should be nothing to worry about apart from a delay in the dispatch of your item.

Contact the seller immediately and ask for a delivery date. If this is too long to wait, ask for a refund and take your business elsewhere. It may be that the seller has a similar item which would be acceptable to you and they could send as a replacement.

How can I ensure that my bid is placed in the final seconds of an auction?

Bidding at the last minute has long been a way to increase your chances of winning an item; the later you make your bid, the less time a rival bidder will have to respond.

There are two main ways to achieve this; the first involves being at your computer as the final stage of the auction draws to a close and then trusting that your broadband doesn't 'go slow' or your computer doesn't crash.

The second way requires the use of some clever software that will place a bid on your behalf in the dying seconds of an auction. There are several companies who offer this service for a small fee (some offer a free service); the process is known as 'auction sniping'.

These are a few of the sites that offer sniping:

- Auction Sniper – www.auctionsniper.com
- Auction Stealer – www.auctionstealer.com
- Just Snipe – www.justsnipe.com

How can I be sure that an auction for music material is legal?

Copying music and video files is much easier with the advent of new technology and it is getting harder to spot the real thing.

Here are some pointers for spotting illegal copies:

- If the packaging looks unprofessional (perhaps a colour photocopy), the chances are that it's not legal.

- CD-Rs, mp3, Real Media and other format files ripped from various web and 'ftp' sites are definitely illegal.

- Bootlegs can include live performances, rehearsals, outtakes and often the record label will not seem official.

- Unauthorised concert recordings released on video and DVD.

TIP

If the item is a 'one-off', contact the seller and ask for more information. If it is a common item check with other sellers and use them for comparison purposes.

Does the timing of my bid really make a difference?

In a word, yes! How and when you place your bid can be a clever buying ploy. Bidding early, for example, will achieve several things:

- Firstly, although the seller cannot actually change the format of the listing to a 'Fixed price' one, they can revise it and add a 'Buy it now' option; your bid will prevent them from doing this.

- The second thing is that your bid, however small, will demonstrate to the seller that there is interest in the item, which may make them think twice about ending the auction early.

They can of course still end the auction early and sell to the highest bidder, or cancel it altogether and re-list at a fixed price.

An early bid will also lock the original auction details, thus reducing the amount of changes that the seller can make. For example, if you notice that the seller has omitted an important piece of information or a key search word, make that bid and they will not be able to amend their auction details; this may in turn reduce the number of hits, and therefore bids, and could bag you a bargain.

One final point about making an early bid – in doing so, you will effectively 'bookmark' the auction without the need to 'watch' it. You can also set your preferences so that you are e-mailed when you've been outbid, helping you keep an eye on the item you're after.

Chapter 3

Deciding What To Sell

Introduction

Selling on eBay can be a great way to make money, and if you fancy a life change it could be a great career move. I am often asked what advice I would give to those new to selling on eBay and the answer is that size matters! Think small in the early days, expand as you gain experience and soon you will have nothing left in the house except the kitchen sink (I have even sold that as well).

What to sell and how to sell it are always key questions; every eBay trader asks them. The following section may well include the question you have been asking yourself.

eBay systems are in place to help make sellers as successful as possible; the more money the seller makes, the more fees they pay and the higher the eBay share price.

Are there certain types of item I should avoid selling?

In my experience almost anything will sell on eBay, from a lock of a pop star's hair to a jar of elephant dung (I was outbid on the latter!) I never cease to be amazed at what actually has a value. As such, there is no reason to rule out anything on the grounds that 'it won't sell'.

There are, however, some products that pose particular problems and these will need to be considered before you decide to sell them.

- **Fragile items**

  Glass, china and collectables can be fragile and their condition is everything to the avid collector. To ensure they arrive safely, you need to spend time and money wrapping and packing them carefully, and the bulkier packaging often means they cost more to post, too (although you can charge P&P accordingly). Consider these implications before you decide whether to specialise in this area.

- **Heavy items**

  Posting heavy items costs more money. Sending heavy items overseas, particularly those with a low sales value, may incur higher fees if you receive payment electronically. This will eat into your profit as the fees are calculated on the total amount of money transferred, including the postage charges.

- **Country specific**

  Selling items that are targeted at only one country will restrict your market. It's better, if you can, to find a product line that will have appeal globally, especially products that the eager foreign buyers cannot buy in their own country. Remember, too, that some items, such as DVDs, may only work in restricted regions.

- **Large items**

  Large items may only be suitable for collection, or may require specialist transportation, which will cost more to arrange.

Consider the implications of any additional packing requirements – will you need non-standard boxes? Can you deliver large items and, if so, within what geographic area? Collection from your home or place of work may be inconvenient and may also restrict your market.

- **High value items**

  The higher the value of your items, the more interest there will be from fraudsters who exploit the system. You are unlikely to be defrauded for a second-hand CD, but a valuable watch might be a target. (There are precautions that can be taken to guard against fraud on eBay, and these are covered in a later section.)

- **Low value items**

  It takes the same amount of time to list an item which sells for £1 as it does to list one that sells for £100. And the time to 'process' the sale is the same too. But the profit on the £100 item will (or should be!) many times higher than the profit on the £1 item. Other things being equal, it's better to specialise in items that are mid to high value than in ultra low-value items. If something is of a low value, or has a small margin, the profit on it may not be enough to cover your time and expenses. Oh, how I wish I'd never bought those 'Thomas the Tank Engine' play rugs!!

What can I do if the market I want to sell in is already saturated?

There are literally millions of competitors out there. eBay can be likened to a huge online department store with each seller owning a stall inside; they run the infrastructure and we sell the goods.

These are my tips for beating the competition:

1   Compete on service as well as price. Feedback is everything for a business seller, so protect it at all costs. Ship your items fast, well packed and for a reasonable cost.

2. Check your competition; find out what they do well and what they don't do so well. Adopt good business practices where possible.

3. Check your competitors' start prices, postage costs, auction start times, policy on returns, payment terms, payment options, and whether they sell worldwide; then review your own activities in light of this knowledge.

4. Cross-sell your items. Could you promote the sale of hi-fi with a plasma TV auction, or a golfing trolley with a set of clubs?

5. Design a clean, sharp eBay presence with no waffle or long Ts & Cs. Make it a desirable place to visit and spend.

6. Stock storage / insurance / the taxman / packing and distribution costs / book-keeping / returns / inventory management / staff / seasonal trading will all need some thought, but all can be mastered.

I believe that eBay is just about to explode in the UK. The number of e-mails I get (and thankfully a few book sales as well!) all point to an undercurrent of interest and we are, after all, a nation of shopkeepers.

Are you allowed to sell promotional merchandise and free gifts on eBay?

As a general rule, as long as the item dispatched is 'as described', eBay are not against this. The seller should state that it is a 'gift with product' in their listing just to ensure that buyers know what the auction is about, something that reduces complaints if nothing else. The eBay policy is:

> *"eBay policy does not specifically prohibit the listing of promotional items, but you should be aware that many rights owners take the position that the listing of such items is a copyright infringement. Listing such items could therefore result in the ending of your listing if a member of our Verified Rights Owner Programme (VeRO) reports the items as infringing their rights."*

This applies more to promotional items than free gifts.

The sale of sample size perfumes does make sense to me as even a small bottle can be of some value, but free DVDs and music CDs from the national press have hardly any resale value. I still have dozens in my cupboards; maybe I'll list them when times are lean.

Is selling shop-branded items allowed?

Absolutely. The seller may have end of line stock from a wholesaler, or perhaps the version currently on sale in the High Street is a newer model. They may of course be buying from the shops at the retail price and taking a gamble that their internet sales will go for a higher price.

Cash flow is important for all traditional retail outlets; at certain times of the year they will make massive reductions in price to recoup their outlay. It is at these times you can pick up a bargain; the post Christmas sales are the time to check out the shops and see what is about.

How can I research the potential market for my products?

There is no substitute for market research; if your chosen product has no interest from buyers, it will not sell and you will lose out. If it is very popular, with many sellers offering the same item, the margins will be very low and you will still lose out. Finding a product with the right ratio of demand versus suppliers is the key to a successful eBay business.

A great feature of eBay is that all transactions are transparent so you can see exactly what has been listed on the site and what did, or didn't, sell. Use the search engines to look for your products, but remember that other sellers may describe the same item in a different way, so vary your search criteria.

My top tips for successful searches:

1. **Use different search words**

   Imagine which words a seller might use to describe their item. Try several different phrases and combinations.

2. **Use specific words instead of general ones**

   A search for plastic bucket will return fewer, more-focused auctions than a search for bucket.

3. **For an even more precise search, state the brand / colour / model of the item**

   To find a 1980's model of R2D2 from the Star Wars films, your search could be: Star Wars R2D2 198* Lucas Films.

4. **Search title and description to get more matches**

   You will get more results by searching in title and description. There are only 55 characters of space in the title box, so sellers often cannot fit all of the key words in and will include them in the description.

5. **Add or remove the letter "s" for more results**

   You will see two different lists of items when you search for cup and cups. Try your search with and without the final "s".

6. **Punctuate correctly**

   Punctuation marks, such as a '-' in T-shirt should only be included in the search if you expect it to be in the item description.

When can I use brand names in my listing?

If you are actually selling an authentic, branded product, then you may use the name in your auction title and description. You can only do so to show the original source of the goods, and you must not imply any authorisation by, or affiliation with, the manufacturer. The latter is a practice that eBay condemns under the title "keyword spamming". For more on this see eBay's policies at:

http://pages.ebay.com/help/policies/keyword-spam.html

Can I sell items that I make at home?

Yes, as long as the item conforms to the eBay rules and meets their listing criteria, it is fine to sell your homemade items. See the Appendix for more information regarding items that are not allowed and those that are 'questionable'.

As with all items for sale on eBay, check to see if anything similar is already being sold, as this should help you put a value on your own work.

Is it possible to sell my house on eBay?

The first thing to understand is that you can't actually sell your house on eBay.co.uk. You can place an advert in the familiar format of a listing, but the transaction is known as a 'non-binding auction'. It is similar to placing an ad in a shop window. When the auction ends, the seller should contact the winning bidder and see if they actually want to proceed with the purchase. This would take place outside of eBay as it does with other house sales that do not involve an estate agent.

Some good news, there are no final value fees associated with the auction, only a flat fee to place the listing / advert in the first place.

Last time I checked, there were 52 listings when searching for 'house' within the residential property category, most of which were for properties overseas – not big business, but an interesting area.

Is it worth waiting until Christmas time before selling toys?

I primarily sell toys and there is no doubt that they do sell in greater quantities and for higher prices in the run up to Christmas. The question is, can you survive until then without selling anything? Christmas is a crazy time; my turnover increases fourfold between mid-September and mid-December and the packing goes on late into the night.

The first three months of the year are not great for toys, so I reduce my volume and focus on selling the more collectable items and buying toys ready for next Christmas. It is also a good time to catch up on some sleep!

The two major problems with holding onto stock until the 'right time' is the impact on cash flow and storage; if these are not an issue then I would be tempted to wait. Some categories, such as the collectables market, are in demand all year round. The trick is to sell a variety of products throughout the year; toys at Christmas, sunglasses in the summer, collectables all year and so on. This is difficult to achieve, and even I am still a long way off.

Chapter 4

Sourcing Products To Sell

Introduction

Finding stock is easy right? You just look up the address of the local wholesaler in the Yellow Pages, make a quick call and they drop it off the next day.

If only it was this easy. Sourcing your stock is likely to take up a significant amount of time and cause the most sleepless nights (apart from filling in your tax return!).

There is no easy way to find stock. You could ask another trader where they get theirs, but I can't print the answer you are likely to receive (there may be children reading). This is the one area that nobody will discuss. You could of course try the phone book or type 'wholesaler' into Google, but be prepared for a few disappointments.

Yet, hard as it is, all eBay traders find a way, though it undoubtedly involves a lot of coffee and shoe leather in the process.

There are of course many sources that may yield a good stock supply; this chapter looks at them in more detail.

Can I find stock on the High Street to re-sell on eBay?

I am always on the look out for High Street shops that are closing down or having 'extreme' sales; there is usually something for the eBay trader.

In the case of toys, go for well-known brands – Playmobil, Thomas the Tank Engine, Lego and so on – as these will always be in demand. I would be tempted to have somebody at home logged onto eBay who could look up actual "sold" prices whilst you are in the shop. Work out your margins before you go, so if a set sells on eBay for an average of £15 and you can get it for £10, consider whether the 50% mark up is enough to cover costs, time, etc.

> A recent success for me from the High Street has been fancy dress costumes, which I buy in the January sales and hold until Halloween. I list them from mid-September to end of October and of course they sell well overseas.

I have found that good quality items can fetch around 75% of 'normal' retail price, so if you can get them at 50%, there should be a margin. Avoid the "tricky to post" items; the risk of damage versus time to pack is just too great.

> **TIP**
>
> The High Street is struggling to keep pace with online shopping and cash flow is key to their survival. If you can, consider buying in the post Christmas sales and holding stock until late September when Christmas starts all over again.

What should I consider before placing an order with a wholesale supplier?

Placing an order with a wholesaler can have a serious impact on your cash flow and needs to be carefully thought out. If you can get the right products at the right price and enough of them, you should do very well indeed. Here are my top ten tips for a successful wholesale purchase:

1 Prices will not include VAT – Ensure that you factor this into any price calculations when working through your margins; expect to pay 17.5% more than the published price.

2 Check for minimum order values – Consider the impact on your cash flow and any storage issues that may arise from a large purchase.

3 Wholesalers often have "remainder" lines that would not sell in retail outlets. Can you sell them? Before placing a large order, do your research, check other sellers and see if the market is there for the product.

4 Are they genuine brands? Ask for a sample before placing a big order.

5 Use current eBay auctions as a benchmark for achievable prices. Check completed listings rather than active auctions and see what they *actually* sold for.

6 Prices do not include carriage. Check with your supplier how much it will cost to ship the items.

7   You may have to provide references – Some wholesalers will require references from your current business contacts and there is bound to be a form to fill in.

8   Mixed lots – As manufacturers often pack similar lines in the same box, be prepared for a delivery that has almost what you asked for. The quantity will be correct, but the particular items may vary each time.

> I have a regular order for Polly Pocket toy sets. There are eight sets in the range, but each time different quantities of each one arrive. This is not a huge problem, but I never seem to have an abundance of the most popular model.

9   Be bold – Your wholesaler will also supply to other traders, so if they have something you like that sells well and is at the right price, buy as much as you can, as it may all be gone when you want to re-order. (Author sheds a small tear over previous missed opportunities.)

10 Cash or account? – There are two ways to pay for your goods, cash or on account. If you want to open an account, be prepared to fill in the forms and provide your bank details.

Is there an easy way to make contact with the right wholesaler?

Obtaining stock at the right price can be the biggest hurdle to a successful eBay business and it's the one area that other sellers will not discuss. Teaming up with a reliable wholesaler is essential in order to grow your business and ensure you never run out of things to sell.

Finding the right wholesaler can be tricky and of course more and more people are catching on to the eBay way of life, (I blame a certain author!) I currently use four wholesalers for different lines and although even I will not let on as to exactly who they are, I will let you know how I found them.

Wholesaler lists

1   Typing "wholesaler" into Google and then ploughing through thousands of search results could be the answer, but it will take a lot of time. Instead, you could type "wholesale list" into the eBay search box and choose from over 400 people who have already done this process. For a few pence they will send you a list of internet links which may just have the information you need. In itself, this will not provide the answer (many of the links within these lists will not work or may direct you to the wrong sites) so be prepared for disappointment along the way, but stick with it.

2   Distributors

    Contact distributors who put their names on boxes. If you spot an empty box on your travels, just jot down the contact number – you never know.

3   Local market traders

    I have also built up a network of suppliers in the local markets, who can supply me with items that still have a margin; buying wholesale from them may pay dividends.

If you do find a good wholesaler, don't forget to let me know the details.

4   The internet is a great source; you can stay in the warm, you don't get wet and somebody will deliver to your door. Check the wholesale category on eBay; this is becoming more populated each year.

5   Check out esources.co.uk, it may save you time and money. They are the UK's largest wholesale directory of UK wholesale distributors, suppliers and products. The really good news is that if you opt for the yearly subscription package (https://www.esources.co.uk/premiumbuyer2.php), you will also receive a complementary copy of 'The eBay Business Handbook'.

How do I find goods on eBay that I can resell on the site at a profit?

eBay is a great place to buy goods for resale. Once you have mastered all the elements of the site, particularly the search engines, you will be well placed to find those bargains.

You will already know what sells in your own area and for what price, so check eBay for sellers who do not know the value of their items, buy them cheaply and resell them in a more professional way. Here are my top five tips for bagging a bargain:

1   Look for sellers who only trade within the UK as they have severely restricted their market place, and their items will not reach high sale prices; great news for you.

2   Find those who do not accept PayPal. (When your search results are shown on the screen, sort by "Payment: PayPal last" and the 'Non-PayPal' items will be at the top.) Sellers who do not accept PayPal will again restrict their potential customer

base, even if they sell worldwide, as overseas bidders will find it more difficult to pay.

3   Buy from sellers who only accept a few methods of payment. Reducing payment options reduces prices and should allow you to pick up a bargain.

4   Bad titles are great when looking for a bargain, search for sellers that have made mistakes in the description of their item – maybe the spelling of a key word is wrong, if so, fewer bidders will find the auction.

> I regularly search for auctions with spelling errors in the title, or rather I used to. Now I use the services of AuctionRemind.com (www.auctionremind.com) for free. They search eBay and send me the results via e-mail, leaving me more time for coffee.

5   Exploit the postage system; contact the seller and ask about discounts for multiple purchases and if they would be prepared to send the item by a cheaper delivery method. This should reduce your overall costs and allow you to bid more than other interested buyers who are expecting to pay higher postage costs.

TIP If you do find an item with a mistake in the title, make a small bid. Once a bid has been placed, the seller cannot revise the title, therefore locking the mistake in and restricting the number of competitors you will have for the item.

Can the eBay systems be better employed in the search for more stock?

Finding stock on eBay can be tricky at the best of times, as many other traders will also be looking for it. However you can increase your chances by using the eBay search engine to its full potential.

The simple search is easy, just type in your key words and all live auctions with these words anywhere in the title will be shown. Click on "advanced search" and you can search for these words in both the title and description of active auctions.

By ticking a box labelled "Completed listings only" you can do the same search on auctions that have finished and see the prices that the items went for. This can be very useful when you are deciding how much to bid.

How about beating the competition by using the "advanced search", with the "Show only Buy It Now" and "Sort by Time: Newly listed" options selected. This will show any items fresh to the market with an instant purchase option.

Wading through search results can take an age and it is boring, so narrow your options with a more selective search. If you place speech marks " " at the beginning and end of a phrase, eBay will search for those words in that order – great for DVD titles. Sometimes it is useful to cut down the number of results by telling the search engine which words to ignore, e.g. "star wars" – (episode,1,one) will return titles with the phrase "star wars", but omit the words in brackets. You can add to the list of words to narrow your search still further.

In a similar vein you can search for a particular item from a number of manufacturers (Pampers, Huggies) +nappies will produce items that only have either "Pampers" or "Huggies" and the word "nappies" in the title.

> The fewer items you have to wade through, the more likely you are to locate a bargain.

Where should I look for sources of second-hand stock?

There are some great bargains to be had in the used / second-hand market, after all this is exactly what antiques are. This type of product can offer very high margins, but as each lot is probably unique, the preparation and listing time can be much longer.

Small ads in the paper, notice boards in shop windows, garage sales and even charity shops have provided items for me over the years; however the highest concentration of potential 'used' stock in one place is still your local car boot sale.

Car boot sales are not for everybody, apart from the early starts and the rain you often have to sift through a lot of rubbish to find a gem and these are becoming few and far between.

However, they do still fill a role within my overall sales strategy. I am very selective in what I buy, drawing on 20 years of seeking that illusive bargain. I look for collectable items, especially vintage toys, which tend to have an all year round demand and fill the void after the Christmas buying frenzy ends. If you strike it lucky and pay the right price, you could get some huge margins; collectors will often pay a fortune for a rare item.

TIP Why not approach a car boot trader and ask them to collect items for you. I trade loads of used Lego, and profits are high, but I don't really want to get up early for it; my buyers do that and I pay them to do so.

The secret is to never to be off duty and to be prepared to take a chance. Not buying anything is the only way to ensure you never buy a bad lot.

Is "drop shipping" a viable option?

Drop shipping can a good choice for an eBay business. The main advantage is that you do not have to buy any inventory (stock) in advance but you can still achieve high margins. The drop-shipper carries the inventory and does the shipping, so no more time-consuming packing and posting. All you have to do is market the product, accept your customer's payment, and pay the drop-shipper. The difference between the selling price and the supply cost is your gross profit. Drop shipping also removes the need for storing stock, space costs money, so this can be quite an advantage.

It all sounds too good to be true, so why isn't everybody doing it? Well, you need to find the right partner since your reputation relies on their shipping standards and dispatch times, and all complaints will be sent to you. You will also need to establish a foolproof method of passing orders to your supplier along with your customer's address details and any special delivery requirements.

How does the eBay Trading Assistant scheme work?

The Trading Assistant scheme can be a great way to find stock to sell on eBay. Basically, the Assistants offer their services as a seller and anyone with goods to sell can approach them to sell on their behalf.

This option is ideal if the owner does not have the time or experience to sell their own items; for a fee you can take away all the hassle from them. The fee is usually a percentage of the final value with an allowance for eBay charges.

Consideration should be given to the practical aspects of the trade, where the item is kept while the auction is in progress, and who is responsible for it during this period.

Trading Assistants will usually set a minimum value for the items they are prepared to sell. This will be an assessment of the potential worth at the end of an auction based on experience.

Type in your postcode and see how many other traders offer a selling service in your area, click on their IDs, read their trading terms and see what services they offer. Most seem to be around 15-20% of the final value, with a minimum figure that could be negotiated depending upon the item.

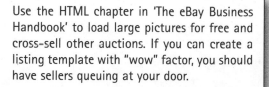

TIP

Use the HTML chapter in 'The eBay Business Handbook' to load large pictures for free and cross-sell other auctions. If you can create a listing template with "wow" factor, you should have sellers queuing at your door.

The full details of the Trading Assistant scheme can be found at:

http://pages.ebay.co.uk/tradingassistants/hire-trading-assistant.html

Are other auction sites a good source of stock to sell on eBay?

Yes. eBay is certainly not the only auction site on the internet, although it is by far the biggest. Depending on the type of items you intend to sell, you may be able to buy from one site and sell on another. Items for sale on other auction sites might not get as many visitors as eBay, so there may be a favourable variation in prices.

As eBay is so competitive, your item may even fetch more money on another site.

Below I have listed some of the other main sites along with their web address. Check them out; you never know what you might find.

QXL – www.qxl.co.uk

eBid Auctions – http://uk.ebid.net

CQout – www.cqout.co.uk

Chapter 5

Listing Items For Sale

Introduction

What makes a perfect listing on eBay? I wish I knew, as I'd be able to retire to the sun. It is a learning curve and quite a steep one at that; spend some time searching on the site to see sellers at every level.

Have you ever stopped to notice how shops on the High Street actually sell you something? They might not appear to be making much of an effort, but simply by placing their products in an inviting way they entice you inside.

Once in the store the well thought out sales plan falls into place and everything from the smell that greets you as you enter the front door to the strategically placed items at the till conspire to ensure you leave a little poorer than when you went in.

Look at your eBay business in the same way: firstly, you must get the customer through the door and then convince them that you have the best overall deal on an item.

This chapter reveals some of the techniques to use in your listings which should increase your customer visits and ensure that when they leave you are a little richer.

When is the best time to end an auction?

A lot will depend upon the type of item you sell and which market you want to address. If you want to entice bidders from the USA, then a time at the end of the day would be more convenient for them as they are 5-8 hours behind us.

For UK sales, I would opt for an end time of between 7pm and 10pm, especially if the item you are selling is for adults. Most children are in bed by ten o'clock, allowing grown-ups time to make those final bids. If you are selling to a younger market, as is the case with my toy sales, it helps if the children are around to twist their parents' arm into one more bid. For them, go for an early evening end time, say between 6-7pm.

As for which day to choose, I have auctions ending on every day of the week and have not been able to analyse which one is best. Always having an item towards the end of the search results list should mean that you get extra hits to your other auctions, providing you cross-sell of course.

Is it possible to do a test run before selling for real?

Yes, it is possible and will currently cost you just 15p. Create a listing and use the scheduling facility, dating it 3 weeks out. When submitted, only you will be able to see the finished article, and you can revise the item as much as you like until you get a look and feel that you're happy with. Then, you can either let the listing carry on, in which case it will go live on the scheduled date, reschedule it for the actual time you would like your auction to start, or cancel it if you just want it to be a practice run.

In what circumstances would you suggest using a reserve price?

There is only one reason I can see for setting a reserve and that is the belief that using this service to kick-start your auction with a lower start price stimulates bidding activity. The reserve price offers a safety net, ensuring that the item is not sold for too low a price. However, reserve prices are not cheap to use, with most items incurring a fee of 2% of the reserve price set.

An item listed with a start price of £29.99 and a reserve price of £100, would currently cost the seller a listing fee of £2.75, whereas starting the auction at £99.99 without a reserve would currently cost the seller £1.50.

A reserve price can only be added at a minimum level of £50.00, so if you see a note on a listing that says "reserve not met", you will know that it has to be at least this amount.

> I do not use reserve prices on any of my auctions. For one thing I am too mean to pay the extra fee, but I also think that if a buyer won one of my auctions but not the item because the reserve was not met, it would not be good for business.

When is it a good idea to invite "Best Offers"?

The "Best Offer" facility allows sellers to invite an offer from potential buyers on fixed price "Buy It Now" listings. This can be ideal if you are not really sure what your items are worth, but don't have the time to run a traditional auction to find out. Using this option allows interested bidders to make an offer, which you can accept or refuse. A clickable link is shown just beneath the "Buy It

Now" button on the listing page. If the buyer is serious about the item, they will have to give a little thought as to the offer they make; there is a limit on the number of offers that can be made for an individual item.

Using the Best Offer option is a useful way to increase turnover when times are slack. Holding out for the full asking price can result in no sales at all, whereas a range of offers may still yield an acceptable margin and welcome cash flow.

If you find the offer acceptable, you can make the buyer the instant winner by accepting their offer. The buyer would then be notified that they have won, and any other interested buyers who made an offer will be notified that the listing has ended. From then on, you'd proceed the same way as you would with any other completed eBay trade.

> I find this feature a great help when selling a new line. The danger with a traditional fixed price sale is that you could list your item with too low a price and it sells quickly. Now you can enter a higher price and see what response comes back from your potential buyers.

TIP

When eBay run a cheaper listing day (10p, 5p, or free), place your "Buy it Now" listings with a high price and invite Best Offers. If it is priced too high, you may well receive an offer, but you may just find somebody prepared to pay the asking price to be sure of winning.

Why can't I find an item I've listed for auction?

This is a common problem. Depending on what the item is, you may experience quite a long delay before it is found by the eBay search engine.

Listings do not appear instantly on the system; they used to take hours, but I now find most of mine can be found after about 10 minutes of making them live. eBay also state that listings may not appear in searches for a short while after an edit; although I have never had a problem with this.

If you still haven't had any success after 15 minutes, try searching for a word or phrase you have included in the title; this should find the item, and is also a good double check in case you made any spelling mistakes.

> My common typing mistake is leaving out the space between two words; this makes an entirely new word, which for some strange reason nobody searches for...

Also check that you have not placed other characters next to one of your words; brackets, exclamation marks and apostrophes may have an impact on the search results.

The guaranteed way to find an item that is definitely on the system is to search for the item number. Just type this into the search box and it should appear. You can find the item number in your listing confirmation email, in your 'My eBay' section, or in the upper right-hand corner of the Item Page.

If you still have no joy after a few hours, check that you haven't inadvertently listed an item that is not allowed on eBay, as some of these will not appear in search results.

TIP Items with obscenities in the description (for example in the track listing of a CD) won't appear in search results.

What should I include in my returns policy?

Having a clear policy for returns is one of the key areas that buyers will look for before they make their purchase. Having the confidence that the item can be returned if unsuitable should encourage the buyer to place their business with you.

eBay offer these words of wisdom concerning refund policies:

"eBay research shows that "difficulty in returning items" is the top most shopping barrier cited by buyers. As a result, sellers offering a no-hassle return policy have an edge on the competition. Typically they sell a higher percentage of their listed items, compared to sellers who do not clearly describe their return policies or do not accept returns."

That's all well and good, but think about the consequences of your returns policy. Do you really want to offer a "try before you buy" service?

If you decide to offer a returns policy, consider the following:

- On what grounds will you allow buyers to return the item? If you offer '100% Satisfaction Guaranteed' with no quibbles, buyers will certainly like it, but you will leave yourself open to a high level of returns. A less liberal policy may be safer.

- Exchange – Will you offer a replacement item and if so, will the original need to be returned?

- Refund – Will you offer cash back or provide a credit note that can be used on your other items?

- Postage – Will you also refund the postage on the item?

- Cost of returning – Who will pay for the cost of returning the item to you? And if you send a replacement item, who will pay the cost of posting that to the buyer?

- Time limit – How long will you allow buyers to return goods? You don't want to sell Christmas decorations in November only to have them returned in February when they may not be quite as popular.

TIP If you do need to make a refund for a returned item, use the PayPal service if possible and reclaim some of your PayPal fees. Claim back your eBay fees via the "Non Paying Buyer" process.

A good returns policy should leave the buyer in no doubt as to the circumstances in which they can return an item, and the potential cost they may incur. As with many aspects of eBay trading, the best starting point is to see what your competition offers with their returns policy, and then adapt the best policies to your own business.

Business sellers have more obligations to buyers under current legislation and their returns policy will have to reflect these.

What are the advantages of listing my item in two categories?

Approximately 25% of all sales are made to bidders who browse the categories for items, so for certain items a second category could prove very worthwhile. eBay currently make a charge for this, but it can increase the number of potential bidders that visit your auction.

Where to use

Second categories should only be used where the item logically fits into more than one, which does require some understanding of what the others categories are. This knowledge can be gained by doing some research. Try using the 'suggested category' search engine or searching for the item yourself. For example, if you are selling a collection of Thomas the Tank Engine trains made by Brio, two categories may be an option. There is a category for Thomas the Tank Engine, which will contain all manner of items within this theme, and there is also a category for Brio, again with a vast array of items. By placing your item in both categories, your item can be found by both Thomas and Brio category browsers.

How can I increase my sales and encourage buyers to spend more with me?

Show visitors to one of your auction listings a selection of your other items for sale without the need to leave that page. Cross-selling is a key sales tool for any retail outlet and it can work on eBay as well. This can be used to great effect and there are a number of ways to achieve this.

- Firstly you could just mention in your description that you have other items for sale and hope that the visitor checks them out. If selling a pair of hiking boots, for example, you could write something along the lines "If these boots are just what you are looking for, please check our other auctions where you will also find a great backpack and selection of walking sticks". To see these items, the potential customer would have to visit your "Items for sale" page and then click on the auction for the backpack, walking sticks, etc.

- The next step is to have this statement with a link to your "items for sale" page next to it, thereby making it easy for the potential buyer to get to your list of current auctions. eBay have already created this link for you, it is just waiting to be used. The official term is an "insert" and it can be included when you write your item description.

- The third way is be to make part of your statement into a direct link to the actual auction. So in the phase we used above, the actual words "backpack" and "walking sticks" will become clickable links, taking your customer directly to the relevant auction. This option does involve some knowledge of HTML codes, but is very simple once you get the hang of it.

- The last method I will mention at this point is very similar to the above, still with a statement containing clickable links, but this time how about also having a small picture of the actual item appearing alongside, so that your bidder can see the walking sticks and can click on the picture and be taken directly to the auction.

These cross-selling techniques should keep visitors for longer, increase traffic to your auctions and potentially drive your sales higher.

Is there a 'best day' for an auction to end?

Much will depend upon the products you are selling and what your target audience are likely to be doing at the time. If you list a family car and the auction ends at 5pm on a weekday, your target buyer (i.e. Mum and Dad) may well be returning from work, sorting out the kids or cooking the evening meal. In this case it is the time *and* the day that counts.

I have found that Fridays are traditionally slow as buyers have other things on their minds; Saturday nights are not good for the same reason.

Sunday evenings have always been very busy in my experience as buyers settle down before returning to work the next day.

National and worldwide events can totally disrupt selling patterns; not much will be sold at 3pm on cup final day. Sporting events as a whole need to be worked around and popular television programmes could put an end to your sales unless you reschedule your auctions.

The most unusual, frequent peak is on a Monday morning; it's not a huge increase in turnover, but is noticeable none the less. Anything to put off starting work again I guess!

What start price should I set when I list an item?

Start prices are one of the hardest things to judge – too high and there will be no interest, too low and you may lose out if you only get one bid. The easy answer is to set the start price at the minimum you would be prepared to accept, so even if you only get one bid you should then be up on the deal. In the case of fixed price listings, work out the required margin on the item and then try it at a higher amount. You may get lucky and sell it, but if not, use the free "Re-list" option and reduce the price.

Do you recommend using the "Want It Now" feature?

The "Want It Now" section of eBay is where buyers ask for an item and sellers supply it.

Would be buyers describe exactly what they want and even what they are prepared to pay. Sellers check these 'wanted ads' and can respond if they have the item listed on eBay. The buyer will then receive an e-mail containing a link to the item.

This service can only be a good thing, both from the buyers and sellers point of view. It is another route to market for your products. In the "Toys & games" section there are nearly 3,000 items wanted, although sadly I don't appear to have any of them!

> I often browse through the "Want It Now" section for fun as I am always amazed by what people are after.

Check it out for yourself at:

http://pages.ebay.co.uk/wantitnow

Does a "Second Chance Offer" have to be for an identical item?

Yes, and no! The Second Chance facility is designed to sell the exact same item to bidders unsuccessful at the main auction. Some items are very similar, but not technically the same; half a kilo of Lego, for example, will have a different variety of pieces, but remains fundamentally the same item.

You can use the Second Chance Offer to contact other bidders with your offer. There is space on the form to enter a message to the prospective buyer, but as there is a chance that they will not notice any comments, it should not be relied upon to point out any minor differences in the items.

You may wish to consider contacting the unsuccessful bidder first, by using the 'Contact member' button. Explain that you have a similar item, describe the differences and state that if they are interested you will send over a Second Chance Offer and some pictures (if required). Go to great lengths to let the would be buyer know that you only intend to trade within eBay as direct contact offering goods for sale could be misconstrued as an attempt to solicit a trade outside of eBay, which is not allowed.

This type of contact could also be interpreted as unsolicited mail, or spam, so use with caution.

What are the pros and cons of trading internationally?

This question actually warrants its own book (hmm, there's an idea for the future). Much will depend upon the type of products you sell, which countries you decide to trade with and how many US dollars in cash you can spend.

The main advantage is of course an increase in your potential customer base, which should push your auction prices higher, increase turnover and ultimately provide you with more profit. An overseas buyer does not have to actually win the item, just taking part and pushing prices higher is enough for me.

I have not found any major disadvantages in trading worldwide and currently send around 15% of my items outside of the UK. This figure used to be a lot higher, however recent changes to search results in the USA has reduced my sales there to zero.

You may experience a few communication problems caused by language barriers. To overcome this, I have a link to a translation site on all of my auctions, which doesn't cost anything and may just cut down on a few e-mails.

Postage costs are higher for overseas sales and therefore PayPal costs will also increase as they retain a percentage of the total monetary value of the trade. The good news is that due to recent changes you can now stipulate a separate insurance option for international sales.

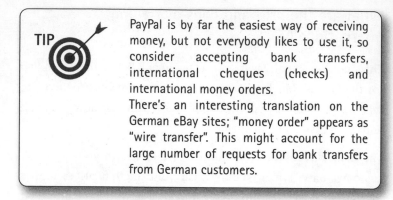

TIP PayPal is by far the easiest way of receiving money, but not everybody likes to use it, so consider accepting bank transfers, international cheques (checks) and international money orders.

There's an interesting translation on the German eBay sites; "money order" appears as "wire transfer". This might account for the large number of requests for bank transfers from German customers.

Should I include all my terms and conditions on each item page?

As a seller, it is important that you convey your trading terms and conditions to all your buyers in order to avoid any unpleasantness at a later date. Ideally, have a link within each auction which takes the viewer to another web page containing your Ts & Cs; however, very few visitors are likely to click through and read them.

As such, having your full trading terms on each auction is almost unavoidable. Make them as easy to read as possible and don't make the font too small – everybody hates small print!

Ts & Cs are a key element when selling on eBay. The payment methods you accept, how long you give buyers to pay, which parts of the world you sell to, and how quick you post your items will all have an impact on your sales.

TIP Check out what the competition offer. If you don't offer the same terms, your sales may suffer.

I have found that a pleasant, friendly environment works best for me. Above all else, keep the amount you write about your terms to a minimum. Include all the salient points, but don't waffle. Buyers will not read the small print and may well become distracted from the main point of the auction.

How does a VeRO warning impact on me as a seller?

This is a standard warning issued when you are about to list an item that has a history of being copied. eBay operates a scheme known as VeRO, where companies who are the 'Verified Rights Owner' of a certain brand, product or phrase can ask eBay to remove your listing.

The warning will appear as below:

"Are you attempting to list a counterfeit item? Are you aware that the listing of such items is not allowed on eBay?

If you continue to list this item, your listing may be removed without notice by the brand owner. If your listing appears to be offering a counterfeit, your listing will be ended and your eBay account could be suspended.

If the item you are offering is authentic, we strongly encourage you to say so in your listing. If your item has a serial number on it, you may include it in your listing. If your item comes with a certificate of authenticity, let potential bidders know that."

As you can imagine the market for counterfeit goods is huge, and this warning is just asking you to check that your item is the genuine article. Every time I list a battery operated train called 'Diesel', I receive a warning as 'Diesel' is also a brand of frequently copied clothing.

If you do get a warning like this, it is always a good idea to revisit your listing and see if you can be more precise about the product: add in details of where it was bought; include a picture of the receipt if you have one; why you are selling it; and so on. If the system suspects that it might be a fake your potential buyers may also have doubts, so put their minds at rest if you can.

> There are loads of companies registered with the VeRO programme and many have written their own 'About me' page to provide further details for buyers and sellers. See the full list at: http://pages.ebay.co.uk/vero/participants.html

Can I list several designs of the same product on one listing?

This is a great idea – on the surface. Give some thought to some of the issues and you might not want to offer this option. From a sales management point of view, it might become difficult to keep track of exactly how much stock you had left. If everybody asked for 'blue shoes, size 7' and you ran out, you would have to stop the auction before the next pair was purchased. It could be a nightmare.

Thankfully it is not actually allowed, so that problem's easily solved. eBay would consider these 'choice listings' to be fee evasion as they would be losing the listing fees for each extra choice option. Place each size and colour variation on a separate, fixed price listing and then cross-sell all the other options.

TIP

The best way to do this is to use an HTML link to a canned search for 'shoes' listed under your ID; all active auctions would then be shown in one list of results.

TIP

When choosing a quantity for each size / colour, keep the total cost just under one of the listing price tiers, this should ensure the most efficient quantity versus price combination.

Does the duration of an auction make any difference to the outcome?

The current options are:

- One day

- Three days

- Five days

- Seven days

- Ten days

Each option has its own advantages. A ten day auction, for example, will allow your auction to run over two weekends and if it starts on a Thursday, which is traditionally a slow day for listings, it will end ten days later on a Sunday, which is generally regarded as the best time for an auction to end. Thursdays are also the most common day for eBay to run a promotion, offering reduced fees, or even a free listing day.

Seven day auctions are the most common; they are easy to track, will include one weekend and allow enough days for more visits, whilst at the same time not asking the high bidder to wait too long for their item. The three and five day auctions are also useful if you believe that most bidding occurs at the end of the auction, with maybe a little activity when the item is newly listed. This would suggest that the duration of the auction is not so important; it is the end time that really counts.

The one day auction is worth a little more explanation, as this can be great under certain circumstances. If you have an item that has a deadline, for example theatre tickets, then the shorter auction will work well. Seasonal events such as Christmas can be a very busy and profitable time for sellers, and the one day format will allow you to make those last few sales before the event and catch the last post before Christmas.

Perhaps the most important use of a one day auction is for those sellers who have many identical items to be sold. eBay will only allow sellers to list a maximum of 15 duplicate auctions at any one time, so if you have 150 DVDs to sell, you can only have 15 listed each week, if you choose the seven day auction. A one day auction will allow you to list 105 items in a week; just start another one when the first one ends.

Ten day versus seven day is really down to personal choice and experience. I usually run ten-day auctions; the simple logic being that the longer an item is in the 'shop window', the more interest it should attract. If I have a lot of identical items then I reduce the duration to shift more products and in the run up to Christmas I try to sell everything I own, so auction length drops towards the big day.

Are eBay shops as good as having your own website?

eBay versus independent websites always causes a big debate. My personal opinion is try eBay first. Commercial websites can cost around £3k each if somebody builds them for you, whereas an eBay shop has nominal start up costs. An eBay shop also has its own URL, which means you can get hits directly from internet search engines as well as from eBay. The eBay brand is also familiar to many online shoppers so trust and navigation shouldn't pose any problems.

How do I ensure that I qualify for PayPal Seller Protection?

The PayPal seller protection policy offers peace of mind to all sellers who qualify and may cover transactions up to a value of approximately £2,500.

To ensure this level of cover applies to your listing, there are a number of requirements that must be met:

- As a seller you must have a Verified Business or Premier account.

- The seller's account must be attached to a bank account that is confirmed through the PayPal Verification process.

- The item must be shipped to an eligible address.

- For a transaction to qualify, the item must be sent to an address identified as 'Confirmed'.

- The item must be tangible goods.

- Only physical items are covered by the Seller Protection Policy. Intangible goods, such as services or items delivered electronically (e.g. software, MP3s, eBooks), are not covered.

- Proof of delivery.

- To file a claim under the Seller Protection Policy, PayPal will need a copy of the proof of delivery; proof of posting will not be sufficient.

- A signed receipt is required for valuable items.

- For items with a value of £125 or more, a signature for receipt is required in addition to proof of delivery.

- Payment for the item must be made in a single transaction from one PayPal account.

- Payments from more than one account for the same item will not qualify.

- The item must be sent in a 'timely manner'.

- To be covered, the item must be shipped within 7 days of receiving payment.

Currently not all countries and regions are covered by the Seller Protection Policy. Check the PayPal website (www.paypal.com) for a current list of those that are included.

How can I entice more visitors to my auctions?

Footfall is important for all businesses; the more people through the door, the more sales that are likely. Having the right goods for sale is not enough, you need the customers to come and look. Here are a few techniques which should drive up your hit rate:

- The title of your auction is the single most important element of the whole listing. Around 75% of buyers find items via the search engine so getting it right is essential. The title space has 55 characters and the trick is to include as many key search words as you can within this limited space to drive as many potential buyers to your auctions. Nobody searches for words like "wow", "cute", "fantastic", "look" and so on, so don't waste valuable space – give your title a little more thought and choose the most appropriate words for your item.

TIP Once you have compiled the best title within the space, take a moment to check the spelling. Searching for mis-spelt words is a great way to find a bargain, but if your spelling is bad, you may not get any visitors.

- Create an 'About me' page and wax lyrical about why you trade on eBay. These pages are free and can be used as an aid to sales, so be sure to include a list of all your current auctions with links to them.

TIP Add a visitor counter to your 'About me' page. Check out www.amazingcounters.com. The counters are free and you can choose from a variety of styles.

- Establish an 'eBay blog'. This is a web diary of your thoughts and interests and you can use it to plug your auctions. These blogs receive numerous hits from the wider internet as they appear on search engine results.

I have an eBay shop. Do I have to 'close' when I go on holiday?

No, you do not have to close in the traditional sense. eBay shops have a great facility known as 'holiday settings', which allows you to state the dates between which packages will not be dispatched. This should ensure that buyers are aware of the delay and can make an informed choice whether to continue with the purchase knowing they will have to wait longer for delivery.

Another option is to make your Shop Inventory listings unavailable while you are away; this will avoid any possible comeback about late delivery, but it also will stop all your sales.

The final decision may depend upon the time you are away from your shop. If it is for a week, buyers should be prepared to wait. If it is a fortnight, maybe a complete shutdown would be best in the long run.

> Be cautious about stating that you will be away from home – just in case the wrong type of person knows where you live.

How should I decide which category to choose when I list a product?

A lot will depend on the item. Generally speaking, the option with the highest 'best match' will suit you as this is where buyers will expect to find this type of item. However, as with all things in life this may not be true all the time. If you choose the third most popular sub-category, your item may stand out from the crowd and attract more interest from browsers. Searchers using key words will find you irrespective of the category you list in.

TIP Make sure you choose a category that applies to your item. Selecting a completely different one misleads buyers and may get you reported.

Chapter 6

Mechanics Of The Sale

Introduction

It's a glamorous life being an eBay trader; coffee breaks whenever you want, a three day working week and no working late (unless you want to).

Well, the coffee break part is right, but much of the time is spent managing the day-to-day processes that are part and parcel of an internet business. This chapter explores some of the fundamentals involved with a sale. Thankfully not every sale needs special attention, most progress without a hitch, however as this selection of questions shows some sales can take a very strange turn.

Why do things sometimes sell for a higher price than in the shops?

The willingness of buyers to pay over the odds has amazed me ever since I started trading on eBay. I regularly buy stock from High Street stores and resell on eBay for a profit, which I think is great. Some of these sales may of course be made to buyers overseas who do not have access to the same products as we do in the UK, and large international companies sometimes release new additions to their range at different times around the world.

This does not account for the sale of a particular item for £20.00 when the same thing is for sale elsewhere on eBay for just £10.00. I have sold items at auction that have reached a final price twice that of the same item that I also sell on a fixed price listing. Buyers can get carried away when they are bidding and do not often stop, take a step back and assess if the item still offers value for money. Instead they stick with the same auction and keep increasing their bid.

It may of course be that some buyers are not able to visit the High Street or don't have access to certain shops where they live. Once you have mastered the eBay system as a buyer, it is quite simple to use, so it may be that these buyers are happy to stay with what they know and pay more rather than search the internet or local shops for the same item. I guess we will never really know for sure.

A buyer in the USA has won my auction even though I said I would only post to the UK – what should I do?

I only sold to the UK in the early days and still have dreams about how much more money I could have made.

Anyway, back to the question. There are a couple of things you can do; the first is to register for a refund of eBay fees via the "Unpaid Item Process":

http://pages.ebay.co.uk/help/tp/unpaid-item-process.html
There is an option here concerning bids from other countries.

Secondly, you could continue with the trade and sell your item to the winning buyer. Check www.royalmail.com for shipping prices to the States, add on a fee for handling and take your first step into global sales.

For future auctions you can block bidders from those countries you do not want to trade with. Check the "Buyer Requirements Preferences" at:

http://pages.ebay.co.uk/services/buyandsell/biddermanagement.html

Why aren't my replies to sellers who ask me questions being received?

When somebody clicks "Ask seller a question", they can choose to hide their e-mail address. When you, the seller, receive the question, you can reply to the e-mail or hit the "respond" button that is within the e-mail itself. The problem arises when you reply and the sender has hidden their e-mail address; your reply will not reach the sender, instead it will disappear into the internet never to be seen again.

eBay do warn you of this in small text, but it is an easy mistake to make. One I still make even now. E-mails that disappear into the internet and never get delivered are sent to an address called "Usetheyellowbutton". To find out how many you have sent that were never delivered, sort your sent e-mails by "To" and scroll down to the e-mails beginning with the letter U. You may be quite upset by what you find – don't even think about the lost sales!

 TIP Use the respond option and you won't go wrong.

If a bidder asks me to cancel their bid, do I have to?

You are not actually obliged to cancel an unwanted bid, but it is generally in your interest as a seller to do so.

It is a pain when this happens and hopefully it's not that often. The bidder can retract their bid at any time as long as there are 12 hours remaining until the auction ends. During the last 12 hours you can still cancel their bid, but they cannot retract it.

The interesting thing in this instance is that if a high bid of, say, £21.00 was removed, the auction price may fall significantly lower than the current second bid of £20.00. It is the third placed bid which then controls the overall price; your second bidder would still be in front, but by only one bid increment over the current third placed bidder.

For example: If the 3rd bid is £4.00, the 2nd bid is £20.00 and the current high bid is unknown, but in excess of £21.00, and that high bid is removed, the price will drop to £4.20; great news for the second bidder, but bad news for you.

There are three things that can be done:

1 Nothing – the high bidder retracts and the retraction will be marked against them for all other sellers to see.

2 Cancel their bid now and hope that interest continues to push the price higher.

3 Cancel the whole auction and start again, blocking the offending bidder.

If the high bidder remains in front and wins the item, they are likely not to pay, which could be awkward. One option is to offer the item to the second bidder at £20.00. If they decline the offer, you could then re-list the item.

Does the style of my listing impact on its success?

There are certain aspects of a listing which I feel are bound to deter buyers, and some that will encourage them. Some buyers prefer pictures, others prefer to read about the item and some will derive an overall opinion about you from the listing as a whole. It is very difficult to cater for all of these variations, but a perfect listing to my mind would include:

- A plain, uncomplicated background with easy to read text (font size 12 or 14).

- Definitely no dancing wizards, background music or animation such as falling snow or stars.

- A clear title reinforcing exactly what is for sale.

- A succinct description, accurate and to the point.

- A few pictures which are in focus and correctly orientated.

- Trading terms presented in a friendly, easy to follow, short format.

- Cross promotion to other items or your eBay shop.

Many sellers employ sophisticated auction templates and for certain items these are fine. I do like the auction listing designers that eBay offer, as they lend a certain level of style.

The layout of an eBay listing is only one factor in its success, obviously feedback, title wording, price and seasonality play a large part as well.

Is the "Featured Item" option really worth the money?

Personally, I am not a big fan of "Featured Plus", but in fairness my average auction price is not high enough to warrant the added cost. I tend to skip the featured section of a category when browsing and move onto the standard listings.

As for a cheaper alternative, I am not aware of one that can replace Featured Plus, but would say that improvements can always be made to improve your visibility. Here are my top five tips for increasing hits:

1   Ensure your titles are as good as they can be, full of key words and 55 characters long (the maximum length).

2   Cross-sell other items from your own listings by using a little basic HTML.

3   Use a gallery for some items, but not all. Sometimes, just sometimes, a more mysterious title such as 'Star Wars Lego set' and no gallery will generate extra hits.

4   Use the sub-title upgrade; this is a much cheaper option and will allow you to write more about your item. The sub-title field is not included in search results, but can still catch the eye.

5   For 'Buy It Now' items, consider an early morning listing time. An item listed at 4am will remain at the top of the list for quite

a while after other auctions have ended, so anybody searching or browsing is more likely to see your item. This doesn't work as well with auction formats as most of the UK will be asleep.

What should I do if another seller copies my pictures or description?

I've experienced this problem from time to time and am actually quite flattered, although it can be very frustrating. Whilst it is perfectly ok to emulate the way in which other sellers conduct their business, using their actual pictures or description without permission is not allowed under eBay guide lines. The section that outlines this can be found at:

http://pages.ebay.co.uk/help/policies/vero-image-text-theft.html

The other seller faces one or all of the following:

- Listing cancellation

- Loss of eBay fees

- Limits placed on account privileges

- Loss of PowerSeller status

- Account suspension

A note to eBay should get the other auction removed and send a warning shot to the seller.

How and when should I use the "Second Chance Offer"?

The "Second Chance Offer" facility allows you as the seller to make a direct offer to any unsuccessful bidders of a completed auction. You can make an offer to the third or fourth placed bidder if the bid price was high enough and, of course, you have enough stock. The great part about is that it does not actually cost anything to make the offer; if the offer is accepted, then a 'final value fee' will apply.

During the process, you will be able to select how many days the offer will remain in place. The under bidder will receive an e-mail with details of the offer, which includes instructions on how to accept it. Just a word of caution, be careful how many days you allow because if you re-list another item straightaway, the bidder may well decide to hold on and see how bidding goes on the new item; wait for the offer period to lapse before listing another.

If any of the under bids are at or above your expected price for the item, then the Second Chance Option is a great way to increase your turnover. It will also negate the need to place a separate listing for the extra items, which means that you can list something else instead.

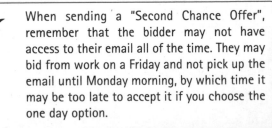

TIP When sending a "Second Chance Offer", remember that the bidder may not have access to their email all of the time. They may bid from work on a Friday and not pick up the email until Monday morning, by which time it may be too late to accept it if you choose the one day option.

Is there an easy way of keeping track of my eBay sales?

Selling on eBay is the easy part – keeping track of all the paperwork can take almost as much time. Check out the "File Management Centre" offered with "Selling Manager" and "Selling Manager Pro".

I hate keeping my accounts up to date (admin has never been my strong point), so the electronic downloading of sold items saves me hours. The data is exported from eBay in a 'comma-separated' (.csv) text file and can be easily loaded by any spreadsheet programme. Just add up the columns and that's your turnover figures sorted.

Just a word of caution, you can only access data for three calendar months, which I discovered when I lost almost all of September 2006. The answer to this is simple; schedule your report downloads and even during the busy times you can keep on top of your paperwork. I just wish it worked out the VAT as well!

How many questions do sellers normally get from bidders?

Questions are great; they show you that your auction is getting some visits. The actual number of questions will vary according to the item; several questions may also suggest that your descriptions are not detailed enough. If these questions have a trend to them, maybe several are payment related, then you should check your descriptions and improve the content if you can.

I decided some time ago to include links within each of my

auctions to a currency converter website, the Royal Mail and one to a language translation service. I am sure these have reduced the number of questions I receive. Another great way to both improve customer service and reduce the time taken to answer questions is to provide answers to the most common ones in your "frequently asked questions" preference; you can find this under preferences in "My eBay". Here you can provide answers to questions such as: "What is your returns policy?"; "Do you combine shipping?"; and "When can I expect my order to arrive?" Your answers will be shown when a potential buyer clicks the "Ask seller a question" button.

Another solution is to write out some standard replies, store them on your computer and then 'paste' them into your e-mail reply. Avoid using HTML as the eBay system doesn't allow it, and other email programmes might view your message as spam.

> One of my eBay virtual friends has stopped answering pre-sale questions altogether and found that sales levels remained exactly the same. I am not really keen on this idea, but it is a thought.

Is trading outside of eBay really that bad?

One of the golden rules when buying anything on eBay is DO NOT TRADE DIRECTLY. eBay will not help you to resolve any problems that might occur. Trading outside of eBay is an example of "fee avoidance", which eBay frown on big time as they lose money. However, it is reasonable for a potential buyer to ask for an outright price and from a seller's point of view any sale is a good sale.

There are several ways round the problem which will keep you onside with eBay, make payment easy and still offer both the buyer and seller protection as normal.

1   If there have not been any bids, you could just revise the item and add a "Buy It Now" (BIN) price.

2   You could cancel the auction, then place another at a fixed price and let the buyer know the item number.

3   If you can't use BIN due to feedback restrictions, create a new auction with the required price as a start price, ask them to bid and then close down the sale, selecting the "Sell to high bidder" option.

Trading outside of eBay will remove all buyer and seller protection, even if the item is paid for using PayPal. It is risky and for the sake of peace of mind not really worth considering.

Can sellers work together and promote each other's auctions?

On the face of it promoting another seller may not seem like the best idea for an eBay business, but certain relationships do work well. If one seller offers golf clubs and another sells golfing umbrellas, then 'sharing' customers makes sense as the buyer may need both items.

Read up on the details in the eBay help page "Cross-Promotion Connections":

http://pages.ebay.co.uk/help/sell/crosspromotion-connections.html

This facility allows other sellers' auctions to be shown under your own cross-promoted items when a bid is placed or an item won.

It is not possible to include direct promotion within an item description – you can only provide links to an eBay ID that is registered in the same name.

If you have an eBay blog, you can of course include links to any seller you choose, just remember to ask them to do the same for you.

Does it matter if my auctions reach much higher prices than my shop?

Not at all, and what a great situation to be in. With auction prices reaching higher levels than your shop listings, I would be tempted to shut up shop and just offer second chances to all under bidders.

I also have this crazy situation, particularly at Christmas when auctions will often outstrip the BIN price for the same item. If you take a step back, you will find that buyers often bid much more on a traditional auction than they can buy the item for at a fixed price. This has a lot to do with the psychology of an auction. Once they are the winning bidder, they feel that the item is theirs, when their bid is then outbid, it becomes personal and they bid again.

> Recently I had a bid of £175 from a lady for 3 "My Little Pony" toys (worth £10) just to ensure she was the winner; she paid promptly and even said thank you.

A great tip is to start auctions as low as possible to get as many people involved early on; they don't tend to look elsewhere and will just stick with the original auction no matter what.

As long as you send the item promptly, well packed, with a polite thank you note inside and give great feedback, you will have completed your side of the transaction.

TIP Make Second Chance Offers within an hour of the auction ending before the bidder finds the item elsewhere.

How can I encourage a bidding war for my items?

If you can list your item in such a way that it appeals to more than one bidding group, then you should see the bids rise to new heights. In the world of toys an example might be 'Star Wars Lego', which appeals to collectors of Lego as well as those interested in the sci-fi films.

Try these ideas in a few auctions and see if you get an increase in bidding activity:

1 Include two or more items in a single listing. Using the example of toys again, try 'Thomas the Tank Engine' and 'Bob the Builder' 'Brio' models. Bidders interested in both areas should find it. Two books on different subjects listed in the same auction could have a similar effect, as each title will entice a different group of bidders.

2 List the combined lot in two eBay categories, thereby enticing more browsers into your auction. There is a fee for the second category and trial and error will establish which items it is viable for.

3 Use the most popular key words for each subject area. eBay

Pulse is a great place to find the most popular search words in each category.

My buyer has paid after I gave them an "Unpaid Item Strike". Can I remove the strike?

This often happens in the case of a buyer who won't pay. When the seller shuts down the trade and reclaims fees from eBay, the buyer is issued with an Unpaid Item Strike; effectively, a bad mark against their record. If they get three of these, eBay will remove them from the site.

It is possible to remove the strike after it has been given; usually you would only do this when you receive cleared payment. Bear in mind that if you do reverse the strike, eBay will recover the final value fee from you as they will deem the trade to have been completed.

Complete the process as follows:

1   Go to "My eBay" and click on "Unpaid Item Disputes".

2   On the "View Dispute" page, select "Cancel the Unpaid Item strike for this dispute".

3   Select "Confirm" if you want to remove the Unpaid Item Strike. The buyer will receive an email confirming that the strike has been removed.

> Remember that a buyer can still leave feedback even if they have an Unpaid Item Strike, so be careful when leaving feedback for them.

Why has my "Buy It Now" (BIN) disappeared?

It is possible to list an item in traditional auction format with the option to purchase it outright for a pre-determined, set price.

In most cases the BIN option will disappear when the auction receives its first bid. The only exception to this is if the auction also has a reserve price in place; in this instance, the BIN will remain an option until the reserve price is met.

> I have found that the bigger the gap between the starting bid price and the BIN, the more likely you are to receive a bid. If you keep the gap to a small amount, the item will probably be sold outright.

What links can I have in my auctions?

eBay will allow certain types of links to be placed within a listing, these include links to extra pictures, terms & conditions, third parties and to your "About me" page. So far so good, however, eBay state that these links "may not include language that promotes items or other websites", so be careful how you word your text.

The links policy concerning the 'About me' page is slightly different to that of a listing page; you can for example link to your own website, eBay Blog or to sites of general interest. Your page "may not contain links to commercial websites where goods from multiple sellers are aggregated by a common search engine", this would include another auction site.

You can check the full eBay links policy at:
http://pages.ebay.co.uk/help/policies/listing-links.html

Is there a way of telling who is looking at my auctions?

Adding a counter is a good idea to determine how many unique visitors you have to your auctions; it can indicate problems with the title or choice of category if you only get a few hits – unless the counter resets, which has been known.

eBay will not release any details about the person who is looking, but there is a software program which builds on the basic counter, called "ViewTracker", which is available from a independent company called Sellathon (www.sellathon.com).

You will have to pay for this service, although there is a 30 day free trail available. Sellathon will give you a better insight to your auction's progress, giving details of:

1 How most eBay visitors find your auctions.

2 What search terms were used to get there.

3 What time (and day of the week) they most often buy.

4 How much time visitors spend looking at your items.

There is a small amount of HTML code that needs to be inserted into your auction description (thankfully all you have to do is paste it in). This will show a more detailed counter on the page and each time somebody visits, data about that visit will be sent to your ViewTracker account.

Why was my item removed from auction on eBay?

eBay don't actually police the site themselves, with most listings being removed following the involvement of other members of the community, i.e. somebody has reported your auctions to eBay.

It could be another seller who has decided to reduce the competition by having your items removed. If so, appeal against the removal and check with eBay that all other aspects of your auctions are correct.

For future auctions, include as many details as possible about the product, where you bought it, how much it was, include a close up picture of any designer label and if possible keep the receipt.

If the brand owner asked eBay to remove your auction, it is because they have reliable information which leads them to conclude that the item listed infringes the company's intellectual property rights. Amongst the possible infringements might be:

- the goods offered for sale are counterfeit or otherwise unlicensed;

- your references to the manufacturer imply that you are offering authentic products when you are not.

Can I reduce the number of emails I get from eBay?

Yes, just go to "My eBay" > "Preferences" > "Notification preferences" and select which ones you still want to receive.

Give some thought to your options before making any changes as the information in these e-mails can often be of great help in managing your eBay sales. Fixed price listing end notifications are a good reminder to keep your stock levels high.

Chapter 7

Postage And Delivery

Introduction

This is a large chapter, which is quite surprising for a subject that, on the face of it, appears to represent such a small part of an eBay trade. However, it is postage and delivery that results in the most complaints from both buyers and sellers. It is this subject which accounts for the majority of e-mails that I receive.

Setting the right postage as a seller will result in a happy buyer. Pack it well and ship it quickly and they may even come back to buy more. If you send the wrong item, badly packed and slowly, then your feedback might not be quite as good.

Some of the questions in this section might appear to be self explanatory and the answers predictable, but just check a few active sellers on the site and see how many still do not follow the basic principles of postage and shipping.

Should I always state my postage charges when I list an item for sale?

You should always include all postage costs, including overseas options if you ship worldwide. There are several reasons why this is a good idea:

1   It will cut down on the number of e-mails you get asking what your postage costs are.

2   It will speed up your payments as buyers will have enough details to pay as soon as they win the item.

3   You will not put off the casual impulse browser who may have an interest in your product, but not enough to be bothered to send an e-mail asking about the postage costs and await your reply.

4   It will encourage you to work out your postage costs and packing requirements prior to listing; this means that you can include any unusual details, such as having to ship in two parcels due to weight restrictions.

5   You will be able to offer a number of postage options, which may have an impact on the buyer's decision; they may be happy to take a slower option to save money.

What do I do if a seller is ripping me off on postage charges?

It is one of the oldest tricks in the book; the item is almost given away, but the postage charges are huge. This is a case of 'fee avoidance' as eBay fees are not paid on the postage element of the trade. There are a few things that can be done:

1 Check to see if the seller is PayPal verified and you are entitled to "buyer protection". This will be shown on the auction page. If they are and you paid via PayPal, open a dispute (there is an option for excess postage charges). I have used this process in the past and it works.

2 Create a second eBay ID to buy with. If you do enter a feedback war over a postage dispute, your selling ID will not suffer and you can vent your annoyance this way.

3 Send an e-mail to eBay expressing your concerns; with a bit of luck they may get time to look into the seller's activities and take action against them.

TIP Always factor in the cost of delivery when making a buying decision and compare the total price with other sellers.

Do I need to post my parcels every day?

Personally, I always take Sundays off, but tend to post items every other day of the week. There are a couple of good reasons for this:

- Firstly, I need the space. The quicker I can move the items, the more room I have.

- The second reason is down to customer care. The buyer has paid, and will want their purchase as soon as possible.

Your personal circumstances will dictate how often you are able to dispatch items. I would recommend adding details of your posting schedule to your terms and conditions. As long as your customers know when the parcel is likely to be sent, they should be fine with this.

Ensure that you keep customers informed, particularly when the item is actually on its way to them; they may have to make plans to be in when it arrives.

Does it cost the same amount to send a parcel to BFPO?

The British Forces Post Office (BFPO) sets the postal rates for sending parcels to members of the armed forces who are overseas. These are the same as for domestic inland first class post. There is not an option to send these parcels by second class, so if you usually quote second class post as your preferred option, you may end up out of pocket.

However, there is one small requirement which differs from the UK inland postal service; one surface of the package must be at least 9cm x 14cm.

BFPO will also deliver your parcel using 'HM Forces Recorded (Signed For)'. The current prices for this service are as follows:

Weight (maximum)	Price including up to £500 compensation for loss/damage	Price including up to £1000 compensation for loss/damage	Price including up to £2500 compensation for loss/damage
100g	£4.30	£4.85	£5.85
500g	£4.75	£5.30	£6.30
1kg	£6.00	£6.55	£7.55
2kg	£7.75	£8.30	£9.30

Are there any alternatives to using Royal Mail for larger packages?

Postage charges are a major element of the overall cost of your item and may well restrict the price it reaches. Bidders like to know the postage charges up front in order to calculate the full cost of the item before they bid.

Recent changes to the Royal Mail monopoly have resulted in more carriers offering their services for parcel delivery. However, this does not necessarily mean that they are a cheaper option.

Here is a small selection of companies who offer this service:

Delivery Networks (www.deliverynetworks.co.uk)

Delivery Networks act as an agent for major parcel carriers – just submit your requirements and you will receive a quote directly from the carrier. Delivery Networks offer:

- Same day services for parcels or documents that need to be sent urgently within the UK.

- Worldwide road and air services. International services are guaranteed, can be tracked and have insurance options.

- Account facilities with leading carriers if your volume of packages is greater than five a day. For smaller volumes use their "Send a Parcel" service, which again can be tracked and has insurance options.

Parcel2Go.com (www.parcel2go.com)

This site offers reduced rates to eBay members with prices starting at £5.75. It also provides packaging advice and the ability to print your own customs documents. Delivery services include:

- Next day delivery within the UK.

- Guaranteed delivery options in the UK before 10am and before 5.30pm.

- International services.

TNT (www.tnt.co.uk)

TNT has a distribution network within the UK and international operations in Europe, Asia, North and South America. They offer:

- An online price calculator to work out a guide price for your shipment.

- Online collection booking services.

- The ability to track your parcel via six different methods.

- Freephone collection booking service.

These companies all offer very similar services; some may provide incentives to eBay members and offer promotions from time to time. Do some research and decide which carrier best suits your needs, and check out the eBay discussion forums for real time comments from other users.

Can I do anything if I inadvertently undercharge buyers for postage?

It happens to us all and if you don't spot it until the last minute, it can prove costly, particularly for a fixed price item. In the case of a traditional auction, a low postage cost may encourage more bids and a higher sale price; this should offset the loss on postage.

If the auction has ended, there is very little that can be done. It may be worth contacting the buyer and explaining the situation – it's a long shot, but they might be accommodating if it's a genuine mistake.

Calculating correct postage costs is important for two reasons: too cheap and valuable profit may be lost, too high and bidders will be put off and may go elsewhere. Give some thought as to the packaging of the item before you even write the description, as this will ensure the costs are correct and you may be able to add a relevant note to the auction, such as "This item will be sent in two packages by parcel post", which really means that you don't have a single box that is big enough, but thankfully have realised this before setting the postage charges.

TIP Consider selecting the postage option "Seller's Standard Rate" instead of "First class / Second class", etc. This will allow you some flexibility with the postage charge, should you need it.

Posting items overseas seems like hard work. Is it really worth it?

Sending parcels overseas is much the same as sending them within the UK; the actual packaging should be the same, although it's a good idea to use better adhesive tape if sending by surface mail as the package is in transit for longer.

The main difference is the information required on the parcel. If you are using an international carrier for large parcels, they will have the necessary documentation, and if using the standard Royal Mail services, a few simple additions to the package will be sufficient.

Generally, the item will be either a "small packet" or "printed papers" – just write the appropriate description in the top left corner and if sending by airmail, add a blue sticker (available from any Post Office).

For parcels sent outside of the EU, a customs declaration (white sticker) is also required. The information on this sticker includes the weight, value and a description of the contents, and you will also need to sign and date the declaration.

A recent change to the design of international eBay sites, particularly the American one, has greatly reduced the amount of items sent out of the UK. However, in my opinion selling internationally is still essential.

Is there an alternative to stamps?

There are several ways to send your parcels; each of them has a cost, whether in time, money or both. A lot will depend on how many you send, how heavy they are and the value of each parcel may also have an impact.

The first step on the postage ladder is of course ordinary stamps, but time spent queuing at the Post Office is money lost. Luckily, there have been improvements on stamps, all of which are available from the Royal Mail:

SmartStamp

- The price paid for postage using this online service is identical to that for postage using stamps, but you don't have to queue at the Post Office and you can also personalise your mail if you wish.

- Printed Postage Impressions

  These offer a simple, pre-printed alternative to postage stamps or franking machines. They are easy to buy and simple to print. PPIs are worth a look if you send a reasonable number of parcels.

- Franking

  Customers benefit from special prices and franked mail costs a little less than standard stamps, but DO you really need a franking machine for your level of business?

- PacketPost

  When you get to a volume of 5,000 parcels per year, PacketPost might be more cost-effective. This service is based on the average weight of your parcels.

You can check out the full details of these options on the Royal Mail website (www.royalmail.com).

TIP Use second class post for the UK and reduce your postage costs; this should make you more competitive.

Should I offer free postage and increase the price of my items?

Offering free postage can be a great sales tool and nobody can accuse you of over-charging for it. There is an option to mark the item with "free postage" in the standard listing form (you can still make a charge for overseas buyers in the normal way).

There is also an advanced search option for finding auctions with "free postage and packing", so this strategy may also increase the number of hits you receive.

The total overall price you can charge for your item will largely depend on what your competitors are doing; you will have to factor in all postage and packing costs when deciding on a price.

eBay love sellers who offer free postage and build additional costs into the selling price as they will receive increased fees from any sale. They have once (to my knowledge) offered a free listing day for items with no UK postage charge.

How do I make a claim for a parcel lost by Royal Mail?

Before considering a claim I would suggest that you ask your buyer to check with their local postal depot in case it is awaiting collection – you may get lucky.

If you obtained a proof of postage, you should be able to claim up to £32.00 from the Post Office. If this was a printed receipt, you should also be able to claim back the postage paid.

The Post Office will ask the buyer to confirm that the package didn't arrive, so let them know that a form will arrive in due course.

An item is not considered "lost" until 15 days have elapsed. If the package has still not arrived after 2 weeks, fill in a "lost, damaged or delayed" claim form which is available from your local Post Office.

You will need to supply the proof of postage, details of the item value and a brief description of the parcel contents. This process takes a long time so keep a copy for your own records as an aide-memoir.

TIP Use the eBay invoice as proof of value, it has always worked for me.

How do I give a buyer a refund if they overpay on postage?

Refunding any over payment for postage via PayPal is a good idea, as you will recover some of your fees along the way. You can issue a partial refund up to 60 days after receiving a payment. You must send the refund by using the "Refund Payment" link, which can be found right at the bottom of the "Transaction Details" page.

If your buyer paid by another method, you could send back stamps instead of money. Returning coins in the post may push the weight of your item into the next postage tier, costing more to send and eating away at any savings.

If I have seriously underestimated foreign postage, can I back out of a sale or charge the buyer more?

Posting heavy items overseas is an expensive business. As a general rule, worldwide airmail is approximately one penny per gram and for Europe its one penny for 2 grams. To make things worse, the most cost effective method is the Royal Mail "small packet" rate, which has a maximum weight limit of 2 kilos.

If you do not realise your mistake until the auction ends, there is very little that can be done. It may be that the reduced shipping costs encouraged the overseas bidder to take part and push the end price higher.

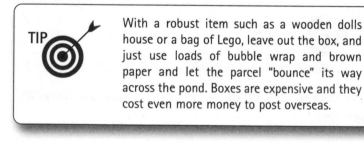

TIP

With a robust item such as a wooden dolls house or a bag of Lego, leave out the box, and just use loads of bubble wrap and brown paper and let the parcel "bounce" its way across the pond. Boxes are expensive and they cost even more money to post overseas.

Which of a buyer's two addresses should I send to – the PayPal address or the eBay address?

Items should only ever be sent to the "confirmed" address as shown on PayPal. Failure to do so will negate any seller protection that may apply.

If the address details are incorrect on eBay, your package may not arrive. This situation is undoubtedly the fault of the buyer who should have updated their records; however, unless you have sent the parcel via a traceable method, PayPal may force a refund. If the buyer files a complaint with PayPal for non-delivery, you must produce "proof of delivery", which of course you would not have.

I would like to offer a postage discount for multiple purchases. How do I do this?

This is a great idea. All buyers hate paying postage charges, so any discount for additional purchases may entice them to stay longer and spend more with you.

The good news is that you should only have to set this up once in your eBay preferences. This kind of postage discount arrangement works best if all the items you sell are approximately the same size and weight, but with a little thought, it should be possible to offer a discount for most items.

How to set up the discounts:

1   Access the "Preferences" section of your "My eBay" page and select the "Postage and discounts" section.

2   Check the box "Apply a postage discount".

3   There are 4 options, so just choose the one that suits best. Option one is, "Charge my highest postage cost for the first item and £*** for each additional item", and all you need to do is add the subsequent postage amount into the box.

4   Save your new settings and carry on with your listings.

My buyer has reduced the postage amount due and then paid; how can I stop this?

This happens quite frequently, and, in my experience, moreso with overseas buyers who bid thinking that the UK postage rates will apply to them. When the invoice arrives with a higher postage charge, they alter it to the figure they had expected and then pay.

Once the buyer has paid, it may not be worth the added hassle to try and recover the additional postage costs.

I used to have this problem a lot, but have now changed my preferences so that my buyers cannot alter the payment details.

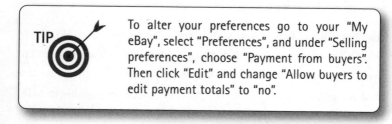

TIP To alter your preferences go to your "My eBay", select "Preferences", and under "Selling preferences", choose "Payment from buyers". Then click "Edit" and change "Allow buyers to edit payment totals" to "no".

Should I offer surface mail as an option for overseas buyers?

Surface mail is a cost effective alternative to airmail, which is approximately half the price. The downside is that delivery may take several months if the parcel is sent outside of Europe.

It is the buyer who must be aware of the issues involved with surface mail. In order to be covered by the "PayPal buyer protection" policy, claims must be filed within 45 days of the payment being made. As surface mail can take longer than this, the buyer may not be covered.

I will send items by surface mail, however I do not offer it as a standard postage option and only send half a dozen parcels per year this way.

What should I do if a "signed for" package is not delivered?

By definition the parcel must be signed for, therefore if it has been delivered, there must be a signature; the question is whose. If there is a signature, you are unlikely to be successful with a claim as Royal Mail has completed their end of the deal.

Report this to the Royal Mail, they will give you a complaint number and then let your buyer know that they are investigating and may be in contact with them. This on its own may result in the parcel suddenly turning up. Signatures are now stored on the website, so it might be worth checking to see if this bears any resemblance to your buyer's name; maybe the package was signed for by a relative or neighbour, who has not told your buyer.

If the parcel cannot be found, you must decide whether to refund your buyer or wait for the case to be resolved. Ensure that your buyer is kept fully informed; if there is a "bad apple" in their neighbourhood, it is in their interest to find out who it is.

Is Royal Mail's ordinary service good enough or should I send my items by recorded delivery?

Sending items via standard mail does run the risk of lost parcels or false claims of non-receipt, but it also costs less. The cheaper you can make your postage, the higher your turnover will be.

If the item is worth less than £32, proof of posting should cover any loss. For higher value items I would recommend recorded delivery or another premium service, just to be on the safe side. If the final price at auction reaches around £50, I will pay the extra cost out of my profits.

The increased sales due from reduced postage costs for your buyers will hopefully outweigh the admin involved in making a handful of claims per year.

> 12 of my domestic UK parcels in the last 5,000 have not been delivered, and they may actually have been lost in the system. All were below the maximum claim threshold.

What exactly constitutes a 'fair' postage charge?

It is fair to incorporate all your packing costs into the postage charges for your item. These would include: all the direct costs, bags, boxes and so on, but could also include an element for labour costs, petrol, and queuing time at the Post Office, etc.

Striking the right balance is tricky; too little and your profits will be eroded, too much and you will deter buyers and may receive adverse feedback. The recently introduced feedback 2.0 system now gives buyers the opportunity to rate particular aspects of the trade, one being postage and packaging charges. If you get the postage charge wrong, your feedback will reflect this.

TIP Check the postage costs of your competitors. How do they compare and does the postage cost impact on the final auction prices?

Chapter 8

Packing

Introduction

It's not a very glamorous subject at the best of times, and for sellers packing can be the worst part of the job. The Catch-22 is that the more successful you become, the more packing you will have to do.

However, it is important, so this chapter includes some of the more exciting questions I have been asked about the subject; sit down before reading as it does get a bit lively in places.

The one piece of advice I would give is to always think twice before you employ a family member to help with the packing; after Christmas when sales slacken off, it's always hard to lay them off.

If you gave some thought to the packing before you listed the auction, you will already know how it will be packaged and should have the materials to hand. If not, how exactly do you arrive at a fair p&p charge and where will you find your packaging supplies?

Can you suggest ways to reduce packing costs?

When you first start to sell on eBay keeping your costs to a minimum is a priority, and actually it remains so for all eBay sellers.

Even with a small turnover, there are a few easy steps you can take that will save you money every time you send a parcel. As your activity increases, you may not have time to use them, but for those first tentative sales, they may just help.

1 Re-use any packaging that is sent to you through the mail. If you buy anything online, keep all the boxes and packing materials and use them to send your parcels. It's great for the environment if nothing else.

2 Pick up odd pieces of bubble wrap when you are shopping. Lots of fruit is shipped in bubble wrap and supermarkets are only too happy to let you have it. This is another way to recycle and your item will take on a pleasant fruity smell.

3 Supermarket carrier bags are a great packing material and don't weigh much. The degradable types of bag are so light, and you end up with so many after a weekly shop, that it would be a shame to waste them. In some parts of the world carrier bag collecting is big business, so you may find that your packing materials are worth more than your item.

4 Get hold of a paper shredder and find a use for all that junk mail that arrives each day – turn that loan application form into protective packing. Paper does weigh quite a lot, so only use this for inland UK parcels.

TIP Use these savings to reduce your postage costs and make you more competitive. Don't use them as a means to increase your profits, as this will just annoy your buyers.

Do you know of a cheap source of packing materials?

I have always been extremely green when it comes to packaging and will recycle anything I can, if it is fit for purpose. Apart from being good for the environment, it is easy on the pocket as an average sized box will cost you around 50p – sell 6,000 items a year and this soon adds up.

When starting out, I would suggest visiting your local shops and supermarkets; they often give boxes away for free!

As your needs grow, trawl eBay for your packing materials. A whole industry has grown to service the needs of eBay traders, with a standard search for 'cardboard box' producing over 500 results. Just type whatever product you need into the search engine and compare prices as you would with any other eBay purchase.

I currently buy my bubble wrap in 200 metre rolls on eBay, delivered to the door for only £12 a roll. Only order three at a time though or you will end up having to sit on it.

For bubble bags of all sizes, I have not yet found a better source than Poundland on the High Street.

Does the packaging of an item really make a difference, or should it just be as cheap as possible?

Unwrapping a parcel is always fun; just think back to Christmas when you were a child. Receiving an eBay parcel is just the same, and if you can exceed your customer's expectations then they are more likely to buy from you again. Taking delivery of their purchase is the last link in the buying cycle and, as a seller, another opportunity for you to impress the buyer.

Every aspect of the package will help form an overall opinion in the buyer's mind. Here are a few things to consider:

- Why not include a 'thank you for your business' note. Use quality paper or card and choose the wording carefully. Look into having these professionally printed as it's not as expensive as you might think.

- Only use clean and sturdy boxes. They can be recycled ones, but remember to remove any labels detailing previous contents.

- Use cost effective, appropriate packing materials for the item you are sending. Polystyrene chippings are great, and bubble wrap, shredded paper and foam all do the job, just ensure you choose the right one for your product.

- Include a waterproof layer if appropriate. Items such as books, clothes, shoes and soft toys can suffer from water damage, and since it always rains in the UK, be prepared and protect your item accordingly.

- Include your return address details. Order some small stickers from a company such as 'Able Labels' (www.able-labels.co.uk).

TIP Why not ask a friend to unwrap a couple of your parcels and let you know what they think. Just remember to wrap them well again before sending on to your buyer!

Do you have any tips for making packing easier and more effective?

Packing, though boring, is one of the most important elements of an eBay trade. I try and coax the kids into helping, but their hourly rate is just too much for me now.

The golden rule is to put yourself in the buyer's shoes and send your item in a way that you would be happy to receive it. By all means use recycled packing materials; I applaud this in any parcels I receive, as I hate waste nearly as much as packing.

Here are my top five for trouble free parcels:

1   Protect fragile items.

2   It sounds like common sense, and it is, but the hassle that broken items can cause is amazing, particularly if they are expensive. Use extra bubble wrap to ensure it arrives intact.

3   Don't send items without a full address including post or zip code.

4   If a parcel can get lost, it will and it always seems to be overseas. Some international addresses are quite complex and we are not used to the format, but get as much information onto the address label as possible.

5   Don't use cheap adhesive tape.

6   Some parcels may be in the system for some weeks, and it has been known for them to start to come apart. I always use better tape for certain destinations!

7   Don't allow items to move within the packaging.

8   Use the correct packaging for the item and make sure it is secure.

9   Don't use inferior or damaged packaging.

10 Avoid cutting corners with your packaging materials. Lightweight boxes and inadequate quality packing could cost you money and the goodwill of your buyer.

TIP Only pack up the item after the auction ends, as buyers may purchase more than one item over a period of days. It would be a waste of time to unpack it in order to send with something else.

I need to buy larger quantities of packing materials. Is eBay a good source?

Packing materials are difficult; you have to buy loads to get a good price and then find somewhere to store them. It gets even worse if you need a variety of sizes to accommodate your items.

eBay is certainly a great place to shop for standard items such as boxes and bubble bags. There is a lot of competition, so shop around.

Boxes

Buying your boxes a few at a time can be very expensive, but if you know that the items you sell are of similar sizes, you should be able to work out the best box size. They will be sent flat, so you will have to assemble them before they can be packed. Last time I checked there were 1,400 active auctions selling cardboard boxes.

Below is an example of what you are likely to pay for 25 of the most popular box sizes.

- Size 127 x 127 x 127mm - £11.00

- Size 203 x 152 x 102mm - £14.00

- Size 305 x 229 x 127mm - £18.50

- Size 279 x 254 x 115mm - £19.00

- Size 432 x 254 x 153mm - £22.00

TIP When sending boxes overseas, cut off some of the flaps to save on weight and therefore cost. The box will remain strong enough and at a penny per gram to the USA, you should save enough for an extra coffee.

Bubble bags

These also come in an assortment of sizes and the bigger they are, the more they cost. Use the smallest bags you can for the type of item (stops the item moving too) and buy in bulk. Consider the new Royal Mail pricing mechanism for 'letter' and 'large letter' options; the use of a larger bag will not only cost more to buy, but now more to send too.

Buying just one bag from a Post Office or retail shop will be very expensive. Instead, check local wholesalers in your area and buy in quantities of at least 100 to get the price of each bag down to a reasonable level. Here is an example of what you are likely to pay on eBay for 100 of the most popular bag sizes along with an idea of what will fit in them.

- Size A (110 x 160mm) Jewellery / watches - £4.70

- Size B (120 x 210mm) Floppy Discs - £6.00

- Size C (150 x 210mm) CDs - £6.50

- Size D (180 x 260mm) A5 size DVDs / Videos - £7.50

- Size E (220 x 260mm) Small Giftware - £10.00

- Size F (220 x 330mm) Small books / software - £14.00

- Size G (240 x 330mm) A4 size brochures / literature - £14.00

- Size H (270 x 360mm) Larger books - £20.00

- Size J (300 x 440mm) Small clothing - £26.00

- Size K (350 x 470mm) A3 size - £29.00

Prices exclude vat and shipping.

Watch out for damp when storing your packing materials. Molly HQ suffered badly during the winter and water seepage resulted in many unusable soggy boxes.

Chapter 9

When Transactions Go Wrong

Introduction

I received a great question from a buyer in the US asking about one of my top quality fancy dress costumes: "Hi, is this a good price?" I replied that "it is a little on the steep side, especially with shipping costs". They have not bought one as yet.

Communication is vital to ensure a smooth transaction, so why are we so bad at it? I think it's because when dealing online we can't see who we are dealing with, they could literally be anybody and it's more difficult to build trust. E-mails hide the fact that, for better or worse, there is another human being at the end of the line.

It's good to talk, or e-mail, even when things go wrong, so don't be afraid to communicate with other members, most of whom don't bite.

Most of the following have happened to me over the years, and I dread to think how much money I've lost in the process. I want to prevent you from making my mistakes. Now I respond quickly to all questions, embrace problems full on, never make mistakes on my listings and always cave in when things go wrong.

Do I have to refund a buyer just because they don't like the item I sent?

This is a very common problem for any internet sale and you do have my sympathy having experienced this myself. My first reaction would be to stand my ground and dispute the reason for the return. However, as a seller, the impact of a negative feedback for any reason does have consequences for future sales. Although it is not the easiest thing to do, I would try to avoid this dispute spiralling out of proportion.

TIP Include your terms and conditions, including refund policy, in your item description to help reduce problems later on.

If you decide to make a refund, there are a few things you can do to soften the impact:

• If possible, make any refund via PayPal and reclaim some of your fees.

• Use the "Non-paying Buyer" process to reclaim your eBay fees. Use the mutual agreement option – you will need the buyer's assistance with this.

• Make a Second Chance Offer to the under-bidder, explaining the situation.

TIP One of the great ways to avoid any potential discrepancies is to use several close up pictures of the key areas of your item.

Business sellers that sell at a fixed price have obligations under the "Distance Selling Regulations 2000". This includes a no quibble, seven day "cooling off" clause.

What should I do if I have received a faulty product?

The first thing to do is email the seller using the internal eBay system. Explain the situation and ask how the seller wants to proceed. I would recommend being pleasant in your first note.

Sellers are generally not happy when things go wrong. As well as potentially losing a customer, the time taken to sort out problems along with the added expense eats into profit margins. Additionally an unhappy customer could result in poor feedback, which no seller wants. You may well be offered a replacement product or a refund, the choice is yours. Sometimes the added cost of funding return postage can result in the seller letting you keep the original item.

If the seller does not refund you or replace the item, instigate a dispute with eBay and/or PayPal.

What is the best way to handle non-paying buyers?

Around 1% of my buyers don't pay for a wide variety of reasons.

When somebody places a bid, they enter into a legally binding contract to purchase the item if their bid is the highest when the auction ends. The same applies if a buyer purchases an item outright using a "Buy It Now" option.

eBay operates an 'Unpaid Item Process' which will allow the seller to reclaim any paid eBay fees and to issue a 'strike' against the buyer (as in the game – three strikes and you're out). When the dispute has been closed, the item can be re-listed and if it sells the second time around, you should also receive a refund on this fee as well. You could of course offer the item to an under-bidder if there were any.

I have never taken further steps against non-payers. Although it is a legally binding contract, none of my items are worth the time to pursue never mind any financial considerations involved.

Be certain to block them from any future auctions and leave appropriate feedback.

What should I do if my buyer goes incommunicado?

Your buyer may simply be on holiday or unable to access their e-mail at the moment, so there may not be a problem. I would hold back from leaving them negative feedback in the short term and just send a reminder e-mail.

It can be very frustrating when communication stops for any reason. One thing to try is an e-mail directly to them and also via eBay; they may both fail to arrive, but a copy will remain in the other party's message box within their 'My eBay'.

If after a reasonable time there is still no response, file a dispute for non-payment with eBay.

I currently use the automated e-mail facility of "Selling Manager Pro". My buyer receives a note when they buy thanking them for their business and advising of ways to pay. When they pay another note is sent, this time thanking them for the payment and advising that shipment will be asap. Finally when the item is shipped and marked as 'dispatched', a third note is sent advising that the item is on its way and inviting them to shop with me again. If payment is not received within 10 days, the system will send a reminder e-mail; I start the "non-paying buyer" process on the 20th day.

A seller has sent me the wrong item. How should I respond?

Your seller may simply have mixed up two orders for similar items and sent the wrong one to you. High volume sellers need very accurate stock control processes, and sometimes these can go wrong.

Contact the seller and explain the situation; if it is a straightforward case of the wrong colour or size, a replacement should be easy for them to arrange. If it was a one off, they may have to recover it from another buyer and send it on to you, which will take some time.

Depending on the feedback of the seller, it should be fine to return the item before receiving a replacement, but you will have to use your judgement on this. Confirm this with the seller who will cover the cost of return postage.

My auction has ended at a much higher price than I expected. Should I worry about this?

If your item reaches a level that you didn't expect, you are either very lucky or there may well be a problem. It is possible that the two high bidders are working together to artificially inflate the final price of the item, ensuring that they win it. Once it has been won, they will ask you to send it to a different address to the one stated on the PayPal payment correspondence. The temptation is to agree to this as the item exceeded your expectations.

If the high bidder is intending to swindle you, the PayPal account will have been hijacked and in time the money paid to you will be recovered; if this happens once you have sent the item, you will have neither the item nor the payment.

Perform all the usual buyer checks detailed in this book and delay sending the item for a few days; scammers are often removed from the site very quickly as a result of another auction.

How can I block bidders that I don't want to sell to?

You can restrict the members who are allowed to bid on your auctions in two ways; one method will block an individual member, the second option is a broad brush approach to a whole segment of the eBay community.

Option 1 – Blocked bidders list

If you know the ID of a member you do not want to sell to, you can add them to your "Blocked bidders list". Anybody on this list will not be able to bid on any of your auctions until you remove them.

TIP Use this option to block anybody who does not pay for an item.

Option 2 – Setting your "Buyer Requirement" preferences

It is possible to block whole sections of eBay from bidding on your auctions; this is controlled in the "Preferences" section of your "My eBay" page and is titled "Buyer Requirements".

The selections you can make are:

Buyers in countries to which I don't ship

This is a great option to block overseas bidders who may not realise that you don't ship to their country.

Buyers with a negative feedback score

Reduce the risk of non-payment by blocking bidders who have a negative feedback score. You can also select how many negatives are acceptable.

Buyers with "Unpaid Item" strikes

If a bidder has received two "Unpaid Item" strikes within the past 30 days, they may not be the kind of bidder you need; here is where you can block them.

Buyers who may bid on several of my items and not pay for them

This setting will restrict the number of items that a particular member can win from you. This is worth considering if you sell expensive items and do not want to run the risk of a buyer not paying for any of them.

Buyers without a PayPal account

As the title suggests, only bidders with a PayPal account will be allowed to participate in your auctions.

Buyers with no credit card on file

You can block bidders who have not placed a credit card on file and then qualify how many feedbacks this block will apply to.

A word of caution

Be cautious about the restrictions you place on your auction listings or you might not get any bids at all. The more requirements you set, the lower your chance of success will be.

> The "Pre-Approved Bidder" feature has been removed for almost all sellers. eBay believe that it was being abused by some sellers and encouraged trades to be completed outside of the eBay system.

How long should I wait before reporting non-payment?

How long you decide to wait for payment may depend upon the type of auction, where the buyer is in the world and how much feedback they have. You may have already settled on a policy which sets out your payment timescales.

The "Non-paying Buyer" (NPB) process is the main vehicle for reporting non-payment. It has one main objective which is to claim back your end of auction fees from eBay. During the process, the high bidder will be sent an email reminding them to pay and informing them of the consequences if they don't. Often this note from eBay will prompt buyers into paying, so it is definitely worth completing.

If your high bidder still does not complete the trade, they will be given a warning from eBay. After three of these warnings, their account will be suspended and they will become "NARU" (not a registered user). If their feedback score was high, this is usually a good deterrent as they will have to start again with zero feedback. If your high bidder has become NARU since your auction ended, you should be able to reclaim your fees straightaway.

> I usually wait until one week after the auction ends and if I have not heard from the high bidder, I will send a polite email asking if all is ok and offering assistance. The high bidder may have forgotten about the item, or be on holiday, so I give them a gentle reminder. If another week passes with no contact, I will begin the NPB process.

What should I do if a buyer wrongly claims that the item I sent him is faulty?

I have steered clear of selling things that are susceptible to go wrong, for just this reason.

There is a possibility that the item was damaged in the post, and I think the only option is to ask them to return it to you. When it arrives, I would then double check that it is definitely the actual model you sent – just in case it has been switched.

If it is faulty, then you should refund all monies, including the return postage costs (I would then consider a claim against the courier for damage in transit).

If you find that the item is in good working order when you receive it, you then have a choice to make; do you cut your losses, re-list it and come to an arrangement with the buyer over postage costs, or return it to the buyer having already agreed that should it be found to be working they will cover the postage to you and back again.

TIP Items such as some computer software require a certain system specification in order to work. If your buyer does not have the correct equipment, then they could view it as being faulty. Double-check your item description in case the user requirements can be refined.

When can I re-list an item after an "Unpaid Item Dispute" on its first sale?

Wait until the "Non-paying Buyer" process has run its course. There is a chance that the buyer may pay up under pressure from eBay, which would save the trouble of listing it again.

The other reason for waiting is that once the dispute is completed, you may be entitled to a refund on the listing fee if the item sells second time around.

It could be awkward if you were to re-sell the item only to have the original buyer pay for it as well.

Chapter 10

Feedback

Introduction

Feedback is a great invention – if you have a decent score. If you have attracted a few comments that are not complementary, then it is flawed and should be changed. Recent changes to the system of rating sellers have resulted in a second feedback mechanism; not only is the seller given an overall 'pass or fail', but now an individual mark in 4 separate areas. Surprisingly the seller cannot rate the buyer in the same way, now that would be revealing.

This chapter looks at some of the more unusual aspects of feedback and some of the most common questions. Whilst I am broadly in favour of the system, even with its flaws, I must temper that with a little caution – don't always believe what you read!

Are you allowed to actually buy or sell 'feedback'?

No, this is definitely not allowed. If you see anything that looks like this, it needs to be reported to eBay as a breach of listing policy.

It does raise an interesting point though, so never rely solely on the actual feedback score; always check a few recent transactions as well. You may find that the seller who is currently selling a new plasma TV has only sold small items up until now. There is a danger that they may have built up a respectable score in order to deceive buyers with a higher value item.

One of the most common ways to buy feedback reads: "For only one penny you can increase your feedback score, just click 'buy it now' and we will leave you a positive feedback. You don't even have to send us the penny. Please don't forget to leave us feedback as well."

Should I leave negative feedback for my seller?

It is always tricky knowing when to leave negative feedback as there is a very real danger that you will receive one as well. Whether it's justified or not, retaliatory feedback is a fact of life – I have only just grown out of it myself.

Contact your seller and explain the problem you have had; they will probably be concerned to find that they have an unhappy customer – most sellers *do* care you know! Your options could include a return and full refund (remember to ask about return postage), partial refund or maybe even a replacement item.

If you do decide to leave a negative feedback, keep your comments factual and related to the item in question. You have up to 90 days in which to leave your feedback, so give it some thought first.

Is it possible to locate negative comments without wading through pages of feedback?

No matter how many positive feedback comments an eBay member has, it will always be the negative ones that generate the interest.

I currently have around 9,500 positive and three negative, and it is always these three that I am asked about.

There is a great free tool on the internet at www.toolhaus.org. Just type in the eBay ID you want to check, select the type of feedback you want to see and the whole history will be shown.

How can I tell if the feedback rating of a seller is genuine?

There are several ways to boost a seller's feedback score, or for that matter a buyer's feedback score. Generally the higher the feedback, the more trust a buyer will have in that seller. On the surface it's straightforward enough as for every successful trade with a unique buyer, the seller's feedback score increases by one. However, it is possible to manipulate feedback to gain credibility before executing a fraud.

Here's how it can be done:

- Feedback fraud. An individual can set up multiple eBay accounts, buying and selling items between the identities and leaving positive feedback along the way to make them all look trustworthy.

- Purchasing feedback. This is a simple case of offering low value items for sale, completing the trade to a high standard and receiving positive feedback. The same works with the purchase of small value items; pay fast and you will receive a good feedback. eBay has started to crack down on this, but it is still rife on the site.

- Buying identities. An eBay ID with a good feedback score is worth money to the fraudsters and they will be prepared to pay for it.

Before you bid, check that the item is typical of others sold by this seller and that the value of items is in the same range. Things get a bit more confusing after three months when it is not possible to see what the trades were for. So if this is the first item offered for sale in the last three months – be cautious.

Why are the feedback scores on eBay all so high?

In a perfect eBay world we would tell each other what we really think about a particular trade. However, the fear of the consequences sometimes prevents us from doing so.

A positive feedback comment will usually receive one by return; the same also applies to neutral or negative comments. The certain way to avoid any blemishes on your own record is to leave only positive scores or none at all. This is why the level of feedback scores is so high.

The new feedback mechanism allows buyers to rate sellers on different aspects of the transaction, including the product, service, P&P & timeliness of delivery. This will give other potential buyers the opportunity to see a more detailed snapshot of the sellers' abilities, if they read it. The great thing about the new system is that the overall comment left by the buyer can be positive, which will result in a positive being left for them. The buyer can express their true feelings anonymously through the detailed ratings.

Feedback is undoubtedly a great aide to sales and does reflect on both the buyers and sellers' track record, but what you cannot see are the thoughts of those who didn't leave any feedback. The system works fine, it is you and me, the members, who may not use it as intended.

As a seller, how can I protect myself from negative feedback?

Unfortunately as a seller on eBay you will not be able to please everybody all of the time; now and again you will cross paths with a buyer who cannot be placated. The most frustrating are those who leave negative feedback without even letting you know that there was a problem.

Negative feedback can be left for a number of reasons, postage is a major cause for complaint, but the item description also causes a few problems from time to time. As a defence strategy against complaints and negative feedback, here are my top five tips to lesson the chance of a negative feedback:

1   Never conceal problems or faults with your item. There is absolutely no point in selling an item, packing it carefully and shipping it knowing that it has a fault. The buyer will spot the problem and return it for a refund, costing you time and money and resulting in an unhappy customer.

2   Take good, clear photographs of the actual item. Do not use stock pictures or representative photographs. Buyers want to see the actual item they will get.

3   Highlight any defects in a clear way. Don't use a small font or bury them within a large block of text. If you do make it clear, this will help in any future dispute.

4   If you have any specific terms and conditions, state them clearly in your item description. This way both parties should know exactly what is expected of them.

5   Clarify your refund policy. Be sure to include timescales for returns and details of any additional postage charges that may apply.

How can I reduce the time I spend leaving feedback?

Feedback is an essential aspect of eBay and some members can become quite upset if it is not left, something that is usually of more importance for those with a lower overall score.

From a volume sellers point of view leaving feedback for hundreds of buyers is a daunting task and one that often gets put to one side; not good for customer relations.

The easiest solution that I have found is to fully automate the feedback processes. This does carry a cost (currently £4.99 per month), as it requires a subscription to the eBay "Selling Manager Pro" sales tool.

Once you have opted for this service, you can leave a pre-set feedback comment for your buyers when they pay, or when they pay and leave you a (positive) feedback. Either way, this facility on its own could save you hours each week – well worth the money.

Chapter 11

Payment

Introduction

Of all the e-mails I receive through my Bulletin, it is the subject of payment that seems highest on sellers' agendas. I can't imagine why. Being paid is not quite as simple as you would expect and eBay do restrict the ways in which it can be done.

PayPal is by far the most widely used payment mechanism on eBay. I deliberately did not use the phase 'most popular' as for many sellers it is a necessary evil which would be replaced instantly if other options were allowed. As the majority of payment transactions use PayPal, much of this section is given over the 'small print' which applies to its use.

However don't despair, there are other ways to be paid and some of them are free to use!

Should I post out items before the buyer's cheque clears?

Cheques are pretty rare these days as around 90% of my payments are made by PayPal. I actually look forward to a cheque payment as it saves money on fees.

Deciding when to send the item is down to personal choice and your view on the buyer; check their feedback, take this into consideration and then decide.

On the few occasions that I have had a cheque bounce, a letter arrived from my bank along with the reason for the return of the cheque. The buyer is likely to incur bank charges of around £25 for each failed transaction, not something they are likely to risk for half a kilo of Lego, but possibly for something more valuable.

> I send items as soon as I receive payment, but that is not to say I would advise anybody else to do likewise. My items are usually of a low value, the financial risks to me are low and during my time selling on eBay I have only had 6 bounces.

Is the seller allowed to charge me more if I pay by PayPal?

Given the option, almost all buyers would use PayPal; it saves on stamps, results in an earlier shipment of the purchase and to some extent offers a degree of buyer protection.

If the seller stated that PayPal could be used, then they must honour this and are not allowed to charge more for PayPal or less for sending a cheque. If they do try to charge more, inform them that surcharging is not allowed and report them to eBay if you still have no joy.

> PayPal costs sellers around 3.5% of the combined final auction price and postage costs. Some sellers choose not to accept it as a payment method and you must accept their terms if you wish to buy from them.

Can I pay for an item with a normal credit card?

Many sellers have 'credit card' listed as a payment option, but unless they have certain banking processes in place they won't be able to accept them. PayPal and similar organisations allow credit cards to be used, but indirectly.

If the seller has the necessary systems in place then you will be able to pay directly with a card.

How do I make an overseas bank transfer?

I have never personally sent a bank transfer out of the UK, all my buying is funded by PayPal for simplicity, however, if you do opt for this method you will need:

1 The seller's name.

2 The name of the seller's bank.

3 Their bank's sort code.

4 Their account number.

In the first instance, check with your bank exactly what the charges are likely to be. I have heard horror stories of £18 fees to send money this way, and understand that different banks have very different charging policies. In addition, ask them to fully explain the process and how long it is likely to take; you may find that a standard cheque payment will be just as quick.

As an alternative, consider using an international money order; this should be a lot quicker and they do have the advantage of being tracked. Check with the seller beforehand.

Two more options to look into are:

1   A direct payment to the seller's credit card account. You would only need the card number, and none of their security details.

2   Visit your travel agent. Many outlets can organise an international transfer of cash instantly to another travel agency or bureau de change in most places. This is a bit more risky and would depend upon how much you trust the seller.

Why is PayPal such a popular payment method on eBay?

PayPal is part of the eBay family of companies, so naturally it will be heavily promoted and advertised as the preferred payment option. Saying that, and despite the fees, I must agree that it does offer the best all round payment option for both buyers and sellers.

The key points about PayPal include:

- It's free for the buyer to use. This encourages more interest as writing and posting cheques takes time and costs the price of an envelope and stamp.

- It is traceable. All transactions are logged and details can be checked long after the trade has been completed.

- Payment is immediate. In most cases, the seller gets their money and the buyer should receive their item quicker as funds do not need to clear.

There are always exceptions to any rule. Some payments via PayPal do need to clear and in certain circumstances payments can be recovered on behalf of the buyer.

- It's convenient for the buyer – just a few clicks of the mouse and the whole process is over.

- Payment is deposited directly into the seller's account. This is great news for any seller's cash flow situation.

- Sellers don't see your credit card details (it's safely encrypted through the PayPal system), which limits the risk of unauthorised use.

- Buyers can be covered up to £500.00 through the PayPal "Buyer Protection Programme". This will depend upon the track record of the seller and is shown on each auction listing.

Should I be worried if my buyer pays with an "eCheque"?

An eCheque is a payment method managed by PayPal, so if you accept PayPal you also accept eCheques. The payment is taken directly from the buyer's bank account and sent to you. It can spend several weeks clearing in the PayPal system and the money is then made available (as with a normal cheque).

As with a cheque in any format, you should not send the item until it has cleared, just in case it bounces. You will receive an e-mail notification of the payment and then another when it has cleared.

eCheques are often generated when a buyer's registered credit card has expired. As such, they may not realise that they have paid with an eCheque, so it is worth letting them know what is happening or they may become concerned as to where their item is.

Should I accept PayPal on my auctions?

The first thing to mention about payment methods is that generally speaking, the more options you give your buyers, the more interest you will have in your auctions. Some people don't have bank accounts or credit cards and what about buyers outside of the UK who don't have access to PayPal? We want to encourage everybody to trade with us, so having as many payment options as possible makes sense.

> The options I currently accept are: PayPal; personal cheque (check) in pounds sterling, euros, US dollars or Australian dollars; UK postal orders; international money orders drawn in pounds sterling or US dollars; and direct bank transfer from the UK and overseas.

From a buyer's point of view, PayPal is so easy to use that if you sell, you will deter bidders if you don't accept it.

When deciding if PayPal is too expensive to offer (assume that you will incur a flat fee per transaction of 20p and around 3.5% of the monetary value transferred), remember that this includes the postage as well. Read more about seller protection at:

http://www.paypal.com/eBay/cgi-bin/webscr?cmd=p/gen/ua/policy_spp-outside

To avoid the expense of PayPal, should I allow payment by bank transfer or cheque?

Bank transfers are great; no fees and once the money arrives in your bank account, it stays there. For buyers in the UK, you will need to supply them with your bank details (name and address), account number and sort code. For buyers elsewhere, you will also need to supply your BIC and IBAN numbers, which will be on your bank statement.

TIP Ask the buyer to cover any charges incurred during a bank transfer and you should be 3.5% up on the deal as there won't be any fees.

Standard cheques have the same advantages as bank transfers in so much as there are no fees to pay (unless you have a business account). The big dilemma with cheques is whether to wait until they clear before sending the item. This is down to personal choice and dependant on the value of the item and trading history of the buyer.

What is a PayPal chargeback?

A chargeback is when PayPal reverse the transfer of money away from the seller back into the buyer's account, even if the item has been dispatched. You can safeguard against this by ensuring that the transaction meets the requirements of the PayPal "Seller Protection Policy".

The two main reasons for a chargeback are:

1 The buyer's account had been used fraudulently by a third party.

2   The buyer has requested a refund of their payment.

Chargebacks are frustrating. I have had only two, and both were for items that were not delivered.

TIP   To avoid the potential for chargebacks, only send to confirmed addresses and obtain proof of delivery – proof of postage will *not* be enough.

Are postal orders worth taking as payment?

This might not be a phrase you hear everyday, but I love the Royal Mail! First they created a very simple pricing structure based on weight and size, which has saved me about 40% on postage costs, and then they breathed new life into the humble postal order.

Postal orders are a 'must have' payment method for all eBay sellers; there are no PayPal fees and no bank charges to pay. You will have to choose when to present them for payment, as nobody likes to queue.

Postal orders have been completely revised; they are now more like cheques and can be bought up to a value of £250. The cost to buy a PO varies from 45p to £8.75 and there is no longer a need to buy multiple orders.

A whole new range of security measures have been introduced, giving added security for the buyer.

Why do I love them so much? Payments by postal order have increased from a couple each month to over 20. More postal orders = less PayPal fees = more profit = more coffee.

How can I send money via PayPal without an eBay item number?

Sometimes there is a need to send money directly from your PayPal account without a corresponding eBay invoice. There may be a need to send a seller additional funds for enhanced postage services or to reimburse a buyer the postage costs of returning an item.

Follow these steps and you will be able to send money to anybody, independently of eBay:

1 Open your PayPal account in the usual way, not via a link in an e-mail.

2 At the top of the page are 5 tabs, click on the one called "Send money".

3 Enter the receiver's e-mail address.

4 Enter the amount, but don't add any currency signs.

5 Select the currency from the pull down menu.

6 Next, select "Goods".

7 Click "Continue" and "Send money".

When is a non-payer definitely a non-payer?

The worst types of non-payers are those who can't make up their mind. If they pay, great, if they don't, at least you know where you stand and can re-list the item. How long you give them is really up to you. I send a polite reminder and then start the non-paying buyer process if they still won't commit either way.

If you do get payment from a buyer who has taken their time, ensure it clears before sending the item just in case there is a problem.

Should I make a refund to a different PayPal account to the one that was used to pay for the item?

I am not keen on the idea of refunding anything to a different PayPal account; for one thing you will not be able to re-claim your PayPal fees.

The original account could have been hijacked which may result in the payment being recovered from your account irrespective of the fact that you credited another account with the money.

I would suggest that you access your PayPal account, find the original payment and make the refund from there, effectively ignoring the request to send it to another account.

Chapter 12

Fees, Duties And Charges

Introduction

I hate paying my fees and naturally would prefer it if eBay let me trade for free and PayPal managed my funds for nothing. As this is unlikely to happen, I have included some of the most popular questions concerning fees and charges that you are bound to come across at sometime in your eBay career.

Surely fees are only paid by eBay sellers I hear you cry. This is not always the case as import taxes can often creep up on you and turn your so-called bargain into an expensive lesson.

Knowing what you should be charged is good business practice, and reducing this figure makes even more sense. Read on for a few fee saving tips.

What constitutes 'fee avoidance' on eBay?

eBay make their money from our fees and will take action against any member found to be avoiding fees through certain activities. These include:

- Offers to trade outside eBay – Doing a deal without the involvement of eBay is not allowed.

- Unreasonable postage or packing costs – As the postage element of a sale does not attract a fee for eBay, items with a low value and high postage charge are not allowed.

- Listings that require additional purchases – Listing an item that requires an additional purchase. eBay quote the example of "travel documents that require the holder to buy or pay for something (such as a hotel room for seven nights) as a condition of receiving the benefit of the coupon (such as free or discounted airfare)".

- Multiple Item Listing (Dutch) Avoidance – Listing a single item and offering additional identical items for sale in the item description. In these situations, the seller typically instructs buyers to indicate the number of items they want, and states that they can get the same price as the item in the listing.

- Email address, phone number or domain name in the title, subtitle or item location –The only exception will be for listings offering a domain name for sale.

- Catalogue sales – Listings of catalogues from which buyers may directly order items are prohibited.

- Reserve fee avoidance – Cancelling bids and ending a listing early because the seller's desired price has not been met.

- Extension of auctions – eBay listings (both auctions and fixed price) have a fixed duration. Extension of the listing duration by a seller, either via the site or the use of automated tools, is not permitted.

Any member found to be in breach of this policy could face one, or all, of the following:

- Listing cancellation.

- Forfeit of eBay fees on cancelled listings.

- Limits on account privileges.

- Loss of PowerSeller status.

- Account suspension.

If I buy items from the USA, will I have to pay import tax?

Possibly, but if your package isn't checked, you may not pay any taxes. Any items brought into the EU (even used items) are subject to two forms of tax; import tax and VAT. Naturally, there are exceptions and HM Customs (http://customs.hmrc.gov.uk) enforce this area.

Any import tax levied against your item will be based on the total value including shipping costs, then the whole lot (item + shipping + import tax) will be liable for VAT; it could get expensive.

The price quoted on the overseas eBay site will not include any elements of tax and as the importer you will be required to pay the extra money.

There are allowances: items under a value of £18.00 can be imported free of tax and those classed as 'gifts' can be sent up to a value of £36.00. There are loads of exceptions including alcohol, tobacco and perfume, so check the HM Revenue & Customs' website and do your sums before you buy.

Has eBay charged me the right amount in fees?

Check the current fee structure at:

http://pages.ebay.co.uk/help/sell/fees.html

If you do the maths on the basis of an overall cost of around 5% of the final value plus the listing fee, you won't be far wrong. If your buyer uses PayPal to settle their bill, you can add another 3.5% of the final fee *plus* 3.5% of the postage charge to your total costs.

Some categories now have a fee of 9% of the final value of the sale. Add this to the costs associated with receiving funds and you could quickly see any profit disappear.

If you suspect that you have been overcharged, contact the eBay help centre. If you think you have not paid enough, keep quiet.

Why has eBay stopped me from listing any more items for sale?

The most likely explanation is that you are behind with the payment of your eBay fees, so eBay have imposed a temporary ban on your selling activities until you clear your slate.

You can build up a total of £15 in owed fees before eBay will take action, and once you pay your dues, the restriction will be lifted.

You don't have to place a credit card on the system if you don't wish to do so; you can make a one-off payment through PayPal or set up a direct debit from your bank account. You can also pay with a cheque or postal order, although these methods take 7 to 10 business days to clear and you will need to send a 'payment coupon' with your payment.

eBay want you to sell as much as possible, as long as you pay your fees of course, so contact them if you are in any doubt.

How do I work out the cost of selling something on eBay?

Current fee structure

The current fee structure of a standard eBay auction is split into two sections.

1   An "Insertion" fee

2   A "Final value fee" (FVF)

These are both described in more detail below. To work out your total costs just add the Insertion fee, along with any upgrade costs, to the expected FVF, which is based on the end price, which of course you cannot be certain about until the auction ends.

1. Insertion fee

You will be charged a fee to actually place your auction on the system. This varies depending on the price your auction will start at. At the time of writing, the range is between 15p and £2.00 for most auctions.

Insertion fees	
Starting or Reserve price	Insertion fee
£0.01 – £0.99	£0.15
£1.00 – £4.99	£0.20
£5.00 – £14.99	£0.35
£15.00 – £29.99	£0.75
£30.00 – £99.99	£1.50
£100 and over	£2.00
For multiple item listings in £100.00 or more tier	£2.00

Different fees are applicable to certain categories; these have lower insertion fees and higher final value fees.

2. Final value fee

eBay will also charge a percentage of the final sale price, the "Final value fee". Again, there is a sliding scale of charges that ranges between 1.75% and 5.25%.

Final value fees	
Closing price	Final value fee
Item not sold	**No fee**
£0.01 – £29.99	**5.25%** of the amount of the high bid (at the listing close for auction-style listings)
£30.00 – £599.99	**5.25%** of the initial £29.99 (**£1.57**), plus **3.25%** of the remaining closing value balance
Over £600.00	**5.25%** of the initial £29.99 (**£1.57**), plus **3.25%** of the next £30.00 – £599.99 (**£18.53**), plus **1.75%** of the remaining closing value balance

Optional feature fees

eBay also offers you a selection of optional upgrades to your basic listing design and for most of these there is an additional, fixed price fee. They currently include:

Reserve fees

Reserve fees (refunded if item sells)	
Reserve price	Fee
£0.01 – £49.99	N/A
£50.00 – £4,999.99	2% of the reserve price
£5,000.00 and up	£100.00

Listing upgrade fees			
Feature	Fee	Feature	Fee
Gallery	£0.15	Highlight	£2.50
Listing Designer	£0.07	Featured Plus!	£9.95
Item Subtitle	£0.35	Gallery Featured	£15.95
Bold	£0.75		
Buy It Now	Variable	Scheduled Listings	£0.06
List in two categories	**Double the insertion and listing upgrade fees**		

Picture service fees

eBay picture service fees	
Feature	Fee
First picture	**Free!**
Each additional picture	**12p**
Picture Show	**15p**
Super-size Image	**60p**
Picture Pack	**1–6 pictures 90p / 7–12 pictures £1.35**

eBay Motors

eBay also have fee structures for selling motor vehicles. Again you will pay an Insertion fee and a Final Value Fee (if the vehicle sells) to list a vehicle on eBay Motors. Currently there is an £8.00 Insertion fee in place and an FVF scale as follows:

Final value fee	
Closing price	Final value fee
£0.01 - £1,999.99	£17.00
£2,000.00 - £3,999.99	1%
£4,000.00 and above	£30.00

In addition to the above eBay fees, money deposited in your account via an electronic method, may also incur a fee. PayPal, for example, charges Premier and Business accounts to receive payments. Personal accounts are free, but cannot receive credit card or debit card payments. The fees are charged to your PayPal account, not your eBay account. More details on these charges can be found in the section concerning payment options.

Free listing days

On occasions, eBay will run promotions and alter or suspend certain payment fees for a day. These take several forms and can result in a considerable saving if you are able to exploit them when they occur.

You won't be given much notice about when these promotions will run, however, they tend to be for auctions listed on a Thursday (traditionally a slow day). These are just a few of the variations that have been used.

- **Free listing days** – No insertion fees will apply.

- **1p gallery days** – The fee for gallery option is reduced.

- **5p listing days** – The insertion fee is reduced.

TIP Take advantage of free listing days that occur on a Thursday. List your item on a ten day auction option which will end on a Sunday and incorporate two weekends.

How can I reduce the impact of PayPal fees on my profit?

Unfortunately you cannot charge a premium for buyers to use PayPal, or reduce the fees if they were to use a different method. You can add a handling / packing charge to your p&p costs, but make it too high and buyers will go elsewhere.

For lower value sales the PayPal charging mechanism eats into any profit. They charge a flat fee of 20p per transaction and then around 3.5% of the money transferred.

As I write there is talk of a PayPal "Micropayments" system with a lower fixed fee and 5% handling charge. This will be ideal for small value transactions.

If you sell an item for 99p and the buyer pays with PayPal, your total fees work out to at least 43% of the sale price. One might suspect that eBay is trying to reduce the number of small sales on the system...

So what can be done? Here are my top 5 tips to reduce those fees:

1   Consider selling in larger quantities; the variable fees will still increase, but the fixed costs will represent a smaller percentage of your overall sales.

2   Recycle as much packing material as possible, but keep your postage costs in line with the competition. These savings will offset the PayPal and eBay fees.

3   Make it *very* clear that you will discount postage for multiple purchases as long as payment is made in one go; this should reduce the number of 20ps you pay.

4   Make full use of eBay reduced listing days; list as many items as you can and use the re-list credits over the coming months.

5   Ensure that you accept as many other forms of payment as possible; check to see if your bank will negotiate international cheques for free, consider international money orders, the humble UK postal order, cash on collection (if suitable), bank transfer and Nochex (which still has a flat fee, but a slightly lower variable rate).

If I list the same item twice by mistake, will I have to pay two lots of fees?

Hopefully you will realise your mistake before both items sell. I have done this only once and it can be tricky to set right.

To cancel the unwanted listing type the item number into the "End my listing early" form, (you can find this via the Help menu at the top of any eBay screen). If your item has already had a bid, you will have to cancel it before you can end the auction, but it is a straightforward process.

Once you have cancelled the offending item, send an e-mail to the eBay billing department (ukbilling@ebay.com), giving them both listing numbers and they should refund you for one of them. For future reference, drink more coffee when listing – it works for me.

How can I find out about eBay's cheap listing days?

The cheaper listing days are announced very late by eBay in order to maintain activity levels in the days prior to the event. Sometimes I get wind of them in time to add a note to my weekly newsletter, so keep an eye on that and check out "Molly's Diary" at www.ebaybulletin.co.uk. They tend to be on Thursdays with a notification sent on the Tuesday.

Will I still have to pay my fees after cancelling an auction?

If the auction is still current at the time you cancel it, you will be charged the original listing fee and any fees for upgrades such as

Gallery. If you subsequently re-list the item and it sells second time around, you should be able to claim back the second listing fee. Any upgrades applied to the second listing will still be charged.

Things are a little complicated if you want to cancel the trade after the auction has ended. You will already have paid eBay both your listing fee and final value fee based on the selling price. To reclaim these fees, you will need the cooperation of the buyer, so ensure that you inform them before requesting a cancellation and fee reimbursement.

Open a Non-Paying Buyer dispute (http://pages.ebay.co.uk/unpaid_item/transition.html) and select the "mutual consent" option.

If the high bidder responds and agrees, you will have your final value fee refunded.

The fees I pay on my eBay sales are so high. Is there a way of reducing them?

Your fees will always be high unless eBay decide to let us all trade for free. Until that time, there are a few things you can do which should reduce the pain a little.

1   Use the tiered starting prices to your best advantage. Start an auction at, for example, £14.99 instead of £15.00. This will currently cost you less in listing fees (check the table above for the price tiers).

2   Multiple, fixed price auctions use the same tiered pricing structure, which is based on the sum of the start prices. You can currently list two items at £7.49 for 35p as the total falls

below £14.99. Three items would cost 75p, so it may be better to run two auctions each with two items for a total cost of 70p.

3   Use the "re-list" option for unsold items; if it sells second time around, the insertion fee is refunded. You can change every aspect of the re-listed auction, so consider a reduction in the start price or vary the listing duration. This option does not apply to multiple items offered using the fixed price Buy It Now format.

4   Use the "Non-paying Buyer" process to reclaim any fees if a buyer does not complete the trade. This is a good tip in itself, however you can also re-list that item for free if it sells the second time.

Chapter 13

Scams

Introduction

Wherever money changes hands there is opportunity for fraud, and eBay is no different. The media will usually focus on the plight of the buyer who has been ripped off by an unscrupulous seller. However, it is not always the buyer who loses out as sellers also run the risk of losing money.

Scams come in many different forms, from the personal invasion of an account hijack to the sneaky return of a subtly different item as 'faulty'. These and many more ploys will be tried to relieve you of your money, product and even your identity.

Fight back against the fraudsters by following some of the advice in this section; never respond via a link in an e-mail and if somebody offers you a brand new X-Box 360 for £50, order one for me as well!

Please don't be put off by this bleak prediction of failed transactions and financial loss as the majority of trades are completed without a hitch. Most traders are honest, but things can go wrong. If you want your experience on eBay to end on a high note, pay particular attention to this chapter.

Loads of items that are not mine have appeared on my selling list. What is happening?

It appears that your account has been hijacked; you need to get help as soon as possible from:

http://pages.ebay.co.uk/help/confidence/isgw-account-theft-reporting.html

This is the eBay help page for hijacked accounts, and they will be able to advise you in real time exactly what to do.

This situation usually arises after providing your eBay account details via a link in a spoof e-mail. It is quite likely that you will no longer be able to access your account as the third party will have changed the registered e-mail address and password.

It must be possible for a seller to inflate the value of their own auction. How will I know if this has happened?

eBay rules state that a seller, any family or friends, must not bid on auctions to artificially inflate the price; eBay call it "shill bidding". This is slightly different to other types of auction where bids can often be placed up to the reserve price of an item.

The most obvious thing to check for is the eBay member IDs that are involved in the bidding; if they are the same few each time then I would be a little suspicious. This is not as easy as it used to be as eBay now protect their identity when bidding reaches a certain level.

There could of course be another reason that bidders are the same each time – maybe the same members tend to be interested in similar auctions and always bid against each other.

Family members and friends are allowed to purchase items using the "Buy It Now" option as these do not involve bidding.

If a member is found to be artificially increasing an item's price, they face suspension and ultimate removal from eBay if they continue.

If you suspect any activity like this, report it to eBay; they will take action if it is required and may even let you know the outcome of their investigation.

Is there any point in reporting a bad seller to eBay?

Yes and no. Many bad sellers are removed, but with false information they can reappear and continue to trade in questionable products very quickly.

eBay cannot police the whole site, there are just too many listings, so they rely on you and me to inform them of any malpractice. There is a link on every listing which allows any of us to report the seller for a whole host of infringements (its right at the bottom of the screen).

Sellers who deal in fake goods can be investigated by Trading Standards, but somebody needs to report them first.

I think I have been conned on eBay. What should I do?

eBay urges buyers and sellers to use both email and the telephone to contact one another to resolve any issues that may arise. You can get the phone number for your trading partner by going to "Find Contact Information" under "Advanced Search". Most issues can be resolved through direct communication between buyers and sellers; quite often it is a simple misunderstanding.

If efforts to communicate directly with your buyer or seller are unsuccessful, consider the following:

- Contact PayPal if this method of payment was used. You may be covered for up to £500.00 by PayPal Buyer Protection.

- If you did not pay through PayPal, contact your credit card company or payment issuer. Credit card issuers typically provide protection in instances of online fraud. Contact your credit card company to learn about the type of coverage and terms they provide.

- Use eBay's "Item Not Received" or "Significantly Not as Described" dispute process.

- Through this dispute process, trading partners are able to communicate online to resolve transaction problems. If problems cannot be resolved, buyers may then submit an eBay "Standard Purchase Protection claim". eBay also reviews "Item Not Received" or "Significantly Not as Described" disputes for possible violations of the "Seller Non-performance" policy.

- Contact the police

To find the contact details for your local police force go to: www.police.uk

I understand that many buyers have been caught out by ticket fraud on eBay. How is this possible?

The sale of tickets is governed by eBay's "Pre-sale Listings" policy:

http://pages.ebay.co.uk/help/policies/pre-sale.html

The main problem with ticket sales for concerts and sporting events is that the tickets are often sold far in advance of the event, but not actually dispatched until a few days before.

When buying a ticket on eBay, you will often be relying on the seller to post you the ticket at some time in the future, but paying them your money now.

Most ticket sellers are fine, but as with all purchases on eBay do your research before you bid or buy.

Problems can occur if the tickets do not arrive and more than 60 days has elapsed (the maximum time allowed to file a dispute under the "Item Not Received" procedure). In this instance, it is quite likely that the seller will no longer be registered with eBay, so there is little they can do to assist.

If you want to pursue it further, you could start legal proceedings against the seller via the small claims court (www.hmcourts-service.gov.uk/infoabout/claims). As with all things there is a leaflet about it.

How can I tell if I have received a genuine eBay e-mail?

'Phishing' (pronounced 'fishing') emails are designed to look as if they come from a particular company and their goal is to fish for your account information. Thousands of these e-mails are sent by fraudsters hoping to catch one or two recipients off guard and then capture their eBay account details. Many of these e-mails will appear to be from eBay.

The fraudsters employ a clever use of an e-mail address, which is often hard to see. An example might be '**@ebayz.com**' instead of '**@ebay.com**'.

There are a couple of quick checks which should help you spot most of these spoof e-mails:

1 Check the 'from' e-mail address. Though on a first glance it may look like a genuine one from eBay, they are often subtly different. Also bear in mind that this can be altered/faked and doesn't necessarily reflect where the e-mail actually came from.

2 Often these emails will contain links that take you to pages on the genuine eBay website to give the e-mail an appearance of being genuine. However, other links in the same e-mail will take you to fake pages made to look like the genuine website. Always check the URL shown in your browser's address bar.

3 Always access eBay or PayPal via their direct web addresses; save it to your favourites to make it quick to get there. Never access your account via an e-mail link.

If in any doubt, ignore the e-mail and check your messages within

"My eBay". Remember to sign in directly to the website and never via a link in an e-mail.

Check out the eBay safety centre and the section on hoax e-mails; there is a great tutorial on how to spot them. Forward any suspicious e-mails to spoof@ebay.co.uk and also to me at mollbol@ebaybulletin.co.uk. I collect fake e-mails and publish them in my weekly eBay bulletin and in "Molly's Diary" on my website www.ebaybulletin.co.uk.

 **TIP** A great way to spot a spoof is by the appalleng spoolling and bad grammir,;.

I have received a "Second Chance Offer". Should I accept it?

A Second Chance Offer is sent by the seller to any under-bidders who have placed a bid that is high enough to provide a sales margin for the seller. Often sellers will have several identical items and make several offers when the auction closes; this saves on listing fees and time.

Recently there has been an upsurge in fake Second Chance Offers designed to obtain your eBay account details. A fake offer will appear to have been sent by the seller and will have all the salient points from the listing; they can look very convincing indeed. Clicking a link on such an e-mail will take you to a spoof eBay site where you will be asked to enter your account details. These fake e-mails are usually targeted at higher value auctions.

If the offer is genuine, then a copy will be in your messages folder in your "My eBay" section, however things may still not be quite right. Some sellers have been known to artificially inflate the price of an auction to find the maximum bid or proxy bid of a buyer. By bidding a ridiculously high amount, the seller will go on to win their own auction and can then send a Second Chance Offer to you at your maximum bid. Although they will have to pay fees on both the original (fictitious) sale and the Offer, the profit margins can be very high.

A reputable seller with a high positive feedback score should be a safe bet as long as the price is acceptable to you. Check back over previous sales and see if there is a trend of selling the same item twice. If in any doubt contact the seller and ask them.

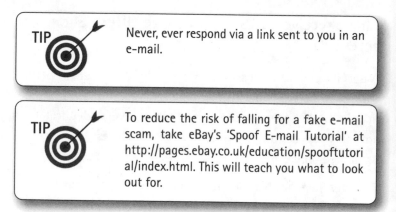

TIP Never, ever respond via a link sent to you in an e-mail.

TIP To reduce the risk of falling for a fake e-mail scam, take eBay's 'Spoof E-mail Tutorial' at http://pages.ebay.co.uk/education/spooftutorial/index.html. This will teach you what to look out for.

Subscribe to my free eBay bulletin at www.ebaybulletin.co.uk and check "Molly's Diary" each day as I print any new spoof e-mails that are sent to me or sent in by other readers.

Why are mobile phone auctions such a target for scammers?

Consumer electronics such as mobile phones, MP3 players and similar items are certainly a target for eBay fraudsters and it is never a bad thing to be suspicious when selling them. The simple answer is that these items are of a reasonably high value and very portable. Although fraudsters can operate anywhere, there does seem to be a tendency for scams to originate from overseas.

These usually operate through the use of hijacked PayPal accounts; you will receive payment in the usual way, but then be asked to send the phone to a different address. In time the PayPal account will be returned to its rightful owner and the funds will be recovered from you.

If you are selling a mobile phone, ensure that you only dispatch it to a "Confirmed address", that is one that has been verified by PayPal and don't send anything to Nigeria. If you are in any doubt about your buyer, send the phone by recorded delivery; even if this is at your own expense, it may be a small price to pay for peace of mind.

This is the classic Nigerian mobile phone scam e-mail:

"Dear Seller,

Am very hilarity to purchase your item. I hope this item is in a good condition because am sending it out as a gift to one of my co-worker who is currently in WEST AFRICA for a products launching that is coming up soon and I will be fully responsible for the postage cost, I would have ask you to send the item to my postal address in United Kingdom but am currently on away due to the daily activities of my work as a chemical importer and exporter researchers that goes around the globally world to introduced and consult the new chemicals that arrived, that is why I need your help to ship this item directly to west Africa. The payment method will be VIA PAYPAL and the postage service will be ROYAMAIL INTERNATIONAL SPECIAL SIGN FOR.

I think the postage cost should not more than this.
Postage Cost: 40.00 GBP
Item Cost: £205.00 GBP
Total Cost: £245.00 GBP

I will make the payment within 24 hours
This is postage address below.

Rotimi Dipo
5 Ipaje Street
Behinds otto kings palace
badagry Express Otto Ijanikin
Lagos state
23401, Nigeria"

My seller is no longer registered; what should I do?

There could be many reasons for the seller being removed. It could be down to outright fraud, in which case they will never be seen again, or it could be down to a minor breach of eBay rules resulting in a temporary suspension. If the seller does not have any blemishes on their record with no negative feedback comments, all may not be lost.

Start the refund process with PayPal now (you can always cancel it if the item does arrive), then e-mail the seller and ask about delivery; even if they have been removed from eBay, they may still honour the trade.

> One of the more innocent reasons for a seller removal is non-payment of fees, and when they are paid the seller is likely to be reinstated. Misleading titles may also result in a temporary ban, as can offering to accept cash as a payment method.

How can I protect my wireless computer network?

Technology is great. Even though I still cannot operate the video '14 day timer', I have managed to encrypt my wireless network. Home hubs and wireless routers are becoming increasingly common and with them comes an increased risk of identity theft.

The first thing to do is ensure that your links are encrypted. Logging into unsecured networks is becoming big business for criminals as it is possible to find out all kinds of information from your web transactions. If you book your holidays online and somebody sees that transaction, they will know when your house is empty. Bank security, credit card details and even your eBay ID and password are at risk.

To set up encryption on your network, access your router's security section and select either WEP or WPA (if all of your hardware supports this protocol). Enter a password or a 32 character string for WEP into your router and then amend the network connections data on each PC (that's four for me at the moment).

Once your network is secure, hackers will have to spend more time breaking your security code and may well just move on to an easier target. They will get in if they really want to, but let's make it a bit harder for them.

Postal fraud must be rife on eBay. What can be done to reduce the risk?

There is no doubt that fraud relating to 'non-delivery' or 'items damaged in the post' is yet another problem sellers have to contend with. Thankfully, it has not been too commonplace in my experience. Items do get lost in the post, especially at Christmas it seems, and sometimes breakages do occur.

I am sure that I have been scammed more than once by this ploy – it is more likely to be 'not received' as a kilo of Lego is pretty hard to damage in the mail.

For higher value overseas items I will often insure the package at my own cost, it's just a case of reducing the risk. Use the Royal Mail 'International Signed For' service which requires a signature on delivery. If an item is damaged, ask for a picture of the problem to help with any claim paperwork at a later date.

For small value items sold overseas, I would be tempted to take the risk and let them go via normal airmail. I have shipped thousands of items this way and only very few ever have any problems. If your item is likely to reach a good final value, or you are selling at a fixed price, add an element of compulsory insurance to the international p&p charges.

When posting within the UK, obtain a proof of posting which will provide some insurance for smaller items and consider additional insurance for more valuable items.

To dissuade possible scammers, include a section in your item description about how the item will be sent. If you intend to send by recorded delivery, a fraudster is unlikely to be able to claim that it was not delivered and may move on to another auction.

Top tips to avoid postal fraud:

1   Obtain proof of postage

It is free and will offer some protection against items that are claimed to be lost. The proof of postage will also show that you did actually send the item.

2   Insist on insurance for high value items

For higher value items, add insurance to your shipping requirements. This will be a relatively small amount in comparison to the value of the item.

3   Ship to confirmed addresses

It is such an important point that it needs to be mentioned again – with higher value items, only ship to the confirmed address.

4   Include a return address

Add a return address on the back of each parcel; there is always a chance that it might find its way back to you.

5   Contact buyer when item sent

As soon as you dispatch the item, notify the buyer. It is great for customer care and will advise them when to expect it.

What will eBay do in the case of fraud?

eBay have an interest in making the site as free from fraud as possible as the threat of being defrauded will deter some people from trading. The scale of the site makes policing every trade impossible; there is just too much happening at any one time. eBay provides the venue for buyers and sellers to come together and trade, they can take action against members who break the rules, but they do rely on the wider community reporting such activity.

eBay state that their goal is:

> *"to create a safe trading environment for our members by facilitating communication and providing services to protect against fraud."*

This means that they will lay down the rules and take action if they are broken.

What eBay does

When suspicious activity is reported to eBay, they will investigate the circumstances and then either warn or suspend accounts that are found to violate eBay policies.

eBay provide the framework and systems that allow buyers and sellers to obtain contact information about each other. Before a trade is completed, it is possible to find out a considerable amount of information on a member and following the completion of a trade, more personal information is made available.

eBay works closely with PayPal to help buyers and sellers resolve their transaction problems. For items paid for with PayPal, members may file a complaint through the PayPal "Buyer

Complaint Process". For all other items, eBay provide the "Item Not Received or Significantly Not as Described" process.

eBay offer a purchase protection scheme and PayPal "Buyer Protection" offers up to £500 in free coverage for qualified items paid for via PayPal.

What eBay does not do

eBay are unable to take action on a member's behalf. This includes contacting another member to ask about the status of an item. They will provide contact information, but will not become directly involved in the dispute.

Since eBay are not involved in the actual transaction, they cannot force a member to live up to their obligation. This also includes pursuing any action outside of the eBay community, which will be up to the individual member to follow up.

I have bought an item directly from the seller, have I lost my money?

Buying an item directly from a seller without using the eBay systems does leave you vulnerable to corrupt sellers. If the payment was made via PayPal, the buyer protection will not be applicable.

If the seller is still trading on eBay and has a good feedback score, all may not be lost. A cheque of any reasonable size will be cleared before the item is shipped, so allow up to two weeks for clearance. Contact the seller and enquire if all is well and when you can expect shipment.

A trade outside of eBay and payment by cheque is very attractive to the seller; with no fees to pay, they should be falling over themselves to keep you happy. Just in case things do not go well, consider another smaller purchase through eBay from the same seller; you will then be able to leave suitable feedback at a later date.

I have been sent a pirate copy instead of the real thing, what should I do?

There are still a lot of fakes sold on eBay; it is a real nightmare for buyers, eBay and the manufacturers of the real thing. E-mail the seller and ask for a refund. I would also want the postage refunded for the return journey if they want the item back. Inform them that selling pirate copies is against eBay rules and that you have been misled.

Things will then go one of two ways. They may well capitulate and make a full refund. If this happens, I would bank the money and then report them to eBay anyway. If they are uncooperative, report them immediately for selling counterfeit goods.

eBay will act on these reports by cancelling listings and removing sellers. Unfortunately these guys will probably just pop up again with a new ID and start all over again.

TIP When buying software, games, designer goods and other items that have a reputation for being copied, be extra cautious. Ensure you check the feedback comments; check their recent trades and how long the seller has been registered as a member.

I am sure that my buyer has returned a different, damaged version of the item I sent them. What can I do?

I am sure that this does happen although I have not experienced it personally as Lego is hard to damage. It is a clever scam and very difficult to prove. The fraudster will already have an item, which is damaged in some way, and then search eBay for one in good condition and buy it.

When the undamaged item is received, it will be switched and the seller told that their item has arrived damaged; they may even accuse the seller of malpractice and threaten bad feedback if the situation is not resolved. As most sellers want to maintain high positive feedback, they are likely to refund the payment, leaving the buyer with an undamaged item free of charge.

This scam may go un-noticed with the seller just putting it down to bad luck, so it is difficult to guess at how many sellers are conned this way. There are a few things that can be done to reduce the risk:

1   For items over a certain value, insist on an element of insurance and send by an 'insured for' service.

2   If damage is reported, check the buyer's feedback and see if this has happened before.

3   For high value items, use an invisible marker and security code it. You could even mention this in your description – hopefully the scammer will move on to another listing.

4   When you leave feedback, mention that the item was returned damaged and replaced or refunded. This will warn others and

may eventually reduce the level of fraud. You can make these comments in a nice way and if the buyer is genuine, they won't take offence.

Chapter 14

Trading For A Living

Introduction

As your experience of eBay grows, you may decide to take your sales to the next level, increasing your turnover and at the same time hopefully increasing your profits. eBay is flexible in this respect, so if you are content with your current level of sales then stick with it, but if you would like to build an empire, then eBay will allow you the freedom to do this too.

It is said that we are a nation of shopkeepers, but can you imagine how big the town centre would be without the internet? Maybe you already have a shop on the High Street and are looking for an additional route to market, or maybe you work on a market and are looking for a warmer option.

When you have successfully traded on eBay, even just once, you have the beginnings of a brand, a name that customers will associate with certain levels of service and product quality.

If the buying experience was a good one, your customers may return to see if you have other items of interest. If things didn't go well, they will soon let you know why. Protect your brand at all costs and build on it where you can; who knows where you might end up.

What are the 'Golden Rules' for sellers?

As with any business activity, trading online has its own strengths. These are my top five tips for a successful venture:

1 Create a pleasant environment for customers to spend their money in.

Nice carpets, soft background music, smiling sales assistants and promotional material all help to create the right atmosphere in which your customer can spend, spend, spend. Online this is more of a challenge; your customer cannot see you, your shop or indeed the merchandise properly. Invest in a good website design, use bright cheerful colours, change the look of your site with the seasons and don't impose harsh trading terms.

2 Accept as many payment methods as possible.

Cash is king on the High Street, as no third party fees make it very welcome indeed. Remember that not everybody has a credit card and asking your buyer to send cash though the post is no longer allowed. Offer as many payment options as possible, don't overlook the personal cheque or humble postal order and ensure PayPal is on your list.

3 Keep your online shop front uncluttered and fast to load.

Broadband has revolutionised the online shopping market and to a certain extent has removed concerns over load times. Customers will move on if your eBay listing does not load in an instant; what was an acceptable delay a year ago is now too slow. Keep the content of your page to a manageable amount and remember that in other countries broadband may not be widely available.

4   Global reach

This has to be the major advantage of any online business; the potential to access most of the developed world and have the world as your customer base. Sure there will be challenges with shipping, language translation and currency fluctuations, but what an opportunity.

5   Establish a robust inventory management system.

With a traditional bricks and mortar shop, your customer cannot buy your product unless it is on the shelf. Poor stock control costs money and the same rule applies online, except that customers can also buy what you don't have. It is very easy to over-stock your eBay shop and not realise the shortfall until it's time to pick the item for shipping.

What happens if I make a loss on eBay?

The first few years in any business can be an uphill struggle and this certainly applies when trading on eBay. The good news is that you can carry forward any losses from the early years until you make a profit.

Assuming you made a loss in year one of £2,000, you could carry this into year two and offset it against any profit you make. If you go on to make £1,000 profit in year two, overall you have still made a loss of £1,000, which can be carried into year three.

As you have made a loss from your eBay business in years one and two, there would be no tax to pay. If year three is better and you exceed a profit of £1,000, then any amount above this may be subject to tax depending upon your personal circumstances.

You will still need to complete a tax return and record all of your expenses in case they are called for. If in any doubt, just call your local tax office; I have always found them to be very helpful.

Why does it cost more to sell something through my eBay shop than by auction?

The fees payable for items sold in an eBay shop include a listing fee and a "Final value fee" (FVF), just as with a standard listing, but they are at different rates to the fees applied to a traditional auction.

Shop items enjoy a lower listing insertion fee, but attract a higher FVF, which is great news if you have the misfortune not to sell anything.

The current fees for "Shop inventory format" (SIF) items are as follows:

Shops Listings Insertion fees

£0.01 – £4.99	£0.03	£0.09	£0.03/30 days
£5.00 – £9.99	£0.05	£0.15	£0.05/30 days
£10.00 – £49.99	£0.07	£0.21	£0.07/30 days
£50.00 – £499.99	£0.09	£0.27	£0.09/30 days
Over £500.00	£0.11	£0.33	£0.11/30 days

Shops Listings Final Value Fees

Item not sold	No Fee
£0.01 – £4.99	10% for the amount of the selling price up to £4.99
£5.00 – £9.99	10% for the initial £4.99 plus 8% of the remaining selling price balance
£10.00 – £49.99	10% of the initial £4.99 plus 8% of the next £5.00 – £9.99 plus 6% of the remaining selling price balance
£50.00 – £499.99	10% of the initial £4.99 plus 8% of the next £5.00 – £9.99 plus 6% of the next £10.00 – £49.99 plus 4% of the remaining selling price balance
Over £500.00	10% of the initial £4.99 plus 8% of the next £5.00 – £9.99 plus 6% of the next £10.00 – £49.99 plus 4% of the next £50.00 – £499.99 plus 2% of the remaining closing value balance

Lower priced items end up with an overall fee of around 10%, whereas an auction running in most eBay categories will have a total fee of around 6%.

In anticipation of trading on eBay for a living, what advice would you give?

My first piece of advice would be to give this some serious thought; trading as a business on eBay is not for everyone. Using the site as a hobby can be great fun, but as a business it can be many other things. It is rewarding, but there is a lot more work involved than you may think. Here are my top 5 suggestions for a more peaceful existence:

1   Separate your business activities from your personal transactions. Mixing the two will be a nightmare to sort out at the end of the tax year.

2   Check if the items you are intending to sell need any special licenses or trading documentation.

3   Keep details of your business transactions and tell the taxman. eBay will not keep these records for you, although they may well let HMR&C know your trading history if asked.

4   Describe your products in an accurate way. Apart from incurring the displeasure of your buyers, you may be liable to penalties under a range of consumer protection legislation.

5   Prepare and update a business plan. Even if it is just on the back of a napkin, have an idea of where you want to be and how you are going to get there. If you don't have a goal, how will you know when you get there?

What should I consider before undertaking an eBay business full time?

Running an eBay business can be very time consuming, especially if you don't have a dedicated space to run it from. Working on the kitchen table is fine for a few items, but is not really the way forward for a business. Much will depend upon the type of item you are thinking of selling, how much spare time you have and how much money you want to make. Here are my top five things to consider before taking the plunge:

1   How big do you want to be? Is it going to be a full-time or part-time operation? How many hours can you devote to it?

Are you thinking about changing careers further down the line and making eBay your main occupation?

2   How much will it cost? You will undoubtedly need some capital to buy stock, maybe even premises or storage space. You will need a certain amount of packing materials in advance of your first sale. Do you have the money for the venture you have in mind?

3   What are you going to sell? Is there actually a gap in the market for your intended products? What competition exists? Are the items seasonal in their appeal or 'flavour of the month'? Can you sustain sales over a longer period of time?

4   Will it actually be worth your while? Run through some figures and work out the likely sales, gross and net profit you think you can make. Remember to factor in all operating costs including purchasing, administration, selling, payment processing and shipping expenses.

5   How will you sell? Do you intend to be a high volume seller taking a small margin or make fewer sales with a higher return on each one? Consider the pros and cons of traditional auctions versus fixed price sales.

Becoming self-employed seems a little daunting, how do I go about this?

Once your activities on eBay have reached a certain level, it may be time to register yourself as self-employed. This will probably occur when you have sold all of your own personal items and decide to begin trading, defined as buying with the intention to sell for a profit.

This can seem complicated and there may be a temptation to continue as before, however the process is not overly difficult and there are some benefits too. Much will depend upon your personal tax circumstances, so check where you stand with the HM Revenue & Customs (www.hmrc.gov.uk/startingup).

What does it mean?

Becoming self-employed on eBay simply means that you intend to buy and sell for profit. As with any earned income, you will need to declare this to HMR&C. It does also mean that any costs involved with your eBay activities can be offset against your profit, as it is the figure after the deduction of these costs that may be liable to income tax.

Self-employment is just the way to capture all the details of your eBay activities and record them in a simple format.

You can be self-employed and also work full or part time. All of your net income is added together and income tax is applied depending on your personal circumstances. If eBay is to be your only source of income, then you can earn up to your personal, tax-free allowance (currently around £5,000), before paying any tax.

The situation becomes interesting if you work full or part time and your eBay activities result in a loss. This loss can, in most cases, be deducted from your employed earnings, resulting in less tax being paid. Make sure you get advice from a tax professional.

How do I register?

The first thing to do is register with HM Revenue & Customs. There is, of course, a booklet about it – "Thinking of Working for Yourself". This contains some basic information and a registration form; just fill it in and return it. The form should be completed within three months of the date you began working for yourself. Alternatively you can access the form online at:

www.hmrc.gov.uk/startingup

HMR&C will then send you a starter pack with more details. This form will also cover the issues surrounding National Insurance contributions.

What advice can you give which would increase sales in my eBay shop?

Items listed in "Shop Inventory Format" (SIF) will not usually show up in general eBay searches so buyers may not even be aware of your existence. Consider the use of standard auction or fixed price listings, which will attract buyers and should drive more visitors into your shop. (Don't forget to cross-sell.)

Check out your competitors and see how they run their business; pay particular attention to their product mix, item descriptions and p&p charges.

Ensure that your returns policy is easy to understand and well publicised in your shop and item descriptions. Business sellers must have such a policy; if yours is too harsh then buyers will move on to another shop.

The design and layout of your shop is also instrumental in its success. Just as a traditional High Street store with a bad layout will deter customers, a poorly designed eBay shop will do the same. Consider these points:

- Ensure that the most relevant product categories are at the top of list and easy to find. If you have a second, smaller, product stream in your shop, group these categories together at the bottom.

- Create a store logo and use this to push your eBay shop brand.

- Entice repeat business with the use of promotions, reduced postage for multiple items and even consider discount vouchers.

- Imagine yourself in the position of a buyer. Would you patronise your own shop?

Are there any practical ways to reduce the amount of administration connected with my eBay business?

I can't believe that you are not a fan of administration; I find it the most satisfying part of the job.

Selling on eBay is quite straightforward and when it's only a few items everything should be fine; you list it, somebody wins it, pays, and then you post it. However, the more you sell, the more questions you will get, you are bound to get complaints along the way, and you may end up permanently attached to your computer keyboard. These are my tips on admin reduction:

- Shipping details: Include these for all locations that you will post to in your description. Provide as many options as you can, including insurance costs if applicable. If you will not post to certain countries, include a note to this effect and make use of the option to block buyers who "Are registered in countries to which I do not post".

- Dispatch details: Keep your buyer informed at all times, and let them know in your item description how long they are likely to wait before their purchase will arrive. Everybody seems to live life in the fast lane and has an expectation regarding delivery; exceed this and you should have a happy customer. Add something like this to your auction listings: "Items will be dispatched as soon as possible after payment. Personal cheques can take up to 7 working days to clear. We aim to post items bought with PayPal on the same day. We will send a confirmation e-mail when the parcel is actually in the post."

- Questions: Include some standard answers to common questions in your "Selling Preferences". This will help to manage your incoming buyer e-mails.

 **TIP** Invest £4.99 in "Selling Manager Pro" and then fully automate your e-mail and feedback systems; this will save you hours each week.

Am I allowed to sell my eBay business and shop as a going concern?

Yes and no. You can sell your stock and business fittings as you would with a traditional business, but you are not allowed to sell your eBay ID. I am not sure where you would stand if you just gave it away.

There is also the issue of any existing customers who have your current e-mail address and contact details. You would either have to give this up or contact every one and inform them of the new details.

There is likely to be an element of 'goodwill' attached to your trading ID, which should increase the value of your business. Seek professional advice before taking the plunge.

How can I generate affiliate revenue from my website?

This arena is huge and can produce significant revenue. Many companies will pay owners of websites a commission for business that is passed to them via links. Almost anybody with a website or Blog can apply to become an affiliate, usually through a third party who will administer the account and payments.

eBay pays a commission for any business passed to them from an external, affiliated website. Check out Commission Junction (www.cj.com) and see if it would be of interest to you.

I have been looking for an alternative to eBay. Is there one?

There are several other auctions sites on the internet, although none have the same volume of trade as eBay. In the UK the second largest is currently www.QXL.com. Others include:

- Amazon Auctions

- Auction.com

- Auctionweiser

- BidItUp

- Buyit Sellit

- Clearance Comet

- CoCo-Bay

- CQout

- Deal of Day

- eBid

- Lucky Bidz

- Morgan Auctions

- P2PBazaar

- QXL

- Sell Your Item

- The Auction Biz

- uBid

- uTrove

- Woocha

Why do certain product lines not sell?

If you have chosen a very popular category, it may be that there is just too much competition. Another reason could be that the size of the market changes throughout the year. Jewellery for example is seasonal, Christmas is huge; the rest of the year, as with toy sales, can be slow.

Here are my top five tips:

1 With most buyers searching, rather than browsing categories, for an item, ensure you use all 55 characters in the title space and squeeze in as many (legitimate) key search words as possible. 'New' is a good one if it applies.

2 Consider the use of a loss leader to stimulate more interest. Try a few auctions with a low start price to increase the hits and then heavily cross-promote your other items.

3 Vary the duration of your auctions; maybe you are missing the busy period with a shorter time span.

4 List your BIN auctions at 4am. This sounds mad I know, but they will be at the top of the list for hours as most competing items are likely to finish before midnight. It will also be good for the US market.

5 Look into the possibility of offering free postage; you may need to increase your sale price, but it would make your item stand out in the search results list.

How can I better plan for seasonal sales patterns?

Christmas is by far my busiest time, but it could be another time of the year if you trade in other lines.

After the summer slump, when bidders are on the beach or outside cremating sausages on the BBQ, comes the scary realisation that Christmas is but a few weeks away. When the children go back to school in September, something happens to the nation's buyers; they all seem to enter a buying frenzy, which is great news for almost all eBay traders.

Coping with seasonality is as much a state of mind as anything else. Here is my top five for surviving Christmas on eBay:

1   Prepare your inventory of items well in advance, stock up well and tailor your items towards Christmas presents. Put away the Dyson spares and find gift items.

2   Take as many pictures as you can during the summer months when times are quieter and the natural light is better. Store these in readiness on your computer.

3   Stock up on packaging materials well in advance. My turnover increases fourfold at this time of year, so having enough boxes and bubble wrap is essential.

4   Anticipate the time it will take to complete the packing and listing. Don't undertake major home improvements over this period and you may even need to take time off work if things get really manic.

5   Recruit additional help; rope the family into some packing duties.

> Using child labour was not a great success for me last time as the deal ended up as "I'll do your packing if you buy me a car". Kids, who'd have them!

Chapter 15

Technology

Introduction

I still have trouble with my video 14 day timer, never mind a DVD recorder; thank goodness for the kids! Setting up an eBay business at home is a lot less daunting and you can be up and running in a few minutes.

My first computer was steam driven and was so old the keyboard only had 22 letters on it. Thankfully things have moved on over the years, and these days I worry about encrypting my wireless network and becoming infected!

Whether you use the internet for buying or selling even if you never even log onto eBay, there are some precautions you can take to ensure safe surfing. This chapter takes a look at the main problems and offers advice on how to combat them.

Technology and a little extra knowledge can save you money, so I touch on the subject of HTML.

Much of the hardware and software required you may already have, it is just a case of getting the kids to put it all together.

What equipment does an internet virgin need to get started?

A lot will depend upon the way you are intending to use the internet and what kind of websites you want to visit. If you want to down load music or films, then a more powerful computer may be needed. These are my thoughts for a general start up package, which will also stand you in good stead should you ever want to start selling on eBay.

1 An up to date computer. These start from about £400 (or cheaper on eBay!) for a desktop model and a little more for a laptop. Older computers will work, but may have some restrictions. It may be worth considering the purchase of a second hand computer if funds are tight.

2 An internet connection. Broadband is not a requirement, but it is now so cheap (at around £15 per month) that not having it can be a false economy – the extra speed is well worth the investment. Dial up connections will cost around £10 per month depending upon your package and service provider.

 TIP Check to see if your home or office can accept broadband at www.broadbandchecker.co.uk.

3 Anti-virus, firewall and other security software; these will help prevent rogue programs corrupting your computer. Some of these programs can be downloaded directly from the internet at no charge.

4 To sell on eBay, you will also need a digital camera, which can be bought for around £70.00.

How can I send automatic emails?

As I write, it will cost you £4.99 per month. This is, in my opinion, one of the best aspects of "Selling Manager Pro", a sales tool supplied by eBay. It offers the ability to have the system send your e-mails for you at predetermined intervals.

The automation preferences can be accessed from your revised "My eBay" screen when you subscribe. You can currently send the following:

1 A winning buyer notification. Use this to elaborate on the payment options you accept and let buyers know about any postage discounts you offer.

2 A payment received e-mail when your buyer pays by PayPal or you mark the item as 'payment received'. This is where you can inform your buyer of the likely dispatch time.

3 A 'your purchase is on its way' e-mail when you mark the item as dispatched. Use this to let your buyers know about your returns policy and thank them again for their business.

You can also send two automated reminder after a pre-set time:

1 A payment reminder e-mail along the lines of "Just thought we would check to make sure you are still ok to buy the item, if we can help in any way, please let us know".

2 A feedback reminder, which is just that; it reminds buyers to leave you feedback.

I currently use all three of the notification e-mails and the payment reminder, which is sent ten days after the auction end. Good communication is very important when you send your money to somebody over the internet; this is the easy way to let your buyers know what is going on.

How can I tell if my computer has been infected with a virus?

The most obvious sign of infection is a slow running machine. It is possibly, but not necessarily, a virus. Unfortunately there are other nasties out there waiting to cause you harm.

As an eBay seller, your computer is your main business tool and should be protected. Install some anti-virus software and run the program at least once a week. There is a huge array to choose from, but AVG is free for home users (www.grisoft.com).

There are three main types of infection which you need to be aware of:

1. Virus

1 A computer virus is a program which has been specifically written to alter the way a computer works. All computer equipment connected to the internet is a potential target for a virus; the operation will take place without the permission or knowledge of the user, and will operate in two ways:

2 It will execute itself, which means it will run without any involvement by you. A virus may also stop other programs from running.

3   A virus will replicate itself. For example, a virus may replace other files with a copy of the infected version.

What to look for

Some viruses are programmed to upset the running of the computer by damaging programs, deleting files, or reformatting the hard disk. Others replicate themselves and make their presence known by presenting text, video, and audio messages without prompting. Even these benign viruses can create problems for the user. They typically take up memory used by legitimate programs. As a result, they often cause erratic behaviour and can result in system crashes. In addition, many viruses are bug-ridden, and these bugs may also lead to system crashes and data loss.

2. Trojan horse

Trojan horses are impostors; that is, files that claim to be something you would like but are in fact malicious. A very important distinction between Trojan horse programs and true viruses is that they do not replicate themselves. Trojans contain malicious code that when triggered cause loss, or even theft, of data. For a Trojan horse to spread, you must 'invite' these programs onto your computers, for example, by opening an email attachment or downloading and running a file from the internet.

One of the worst types of Trojan horse is a program that claims to rid your computer of viruses but instead will introduce them onto your system.

The term 'Trojan' comes from the Greek story of the Trojan War, in which the Greeks gave a giant wooden horse to their foes, the Trojans, as a peace offering. After the Trojans drag the horse inside their city walls, Greek soldiers emerge from the horse's hollow belly and open the city gates, allowing their army to enter and capture Troy. Somebody should make a film about it...

3. Worms

Worms are programs that replicate themselves from system to system without the use of a host file. This is in contrast to viruses, which require the spreading of an infected host file. Although worms generally exist inside other files, often Word or Excel documents, there is a difference between how worms and viruses use the host file. Usually the worm will release a document that already has the worm macro inside the document. The entire document will travel from computer to computer, so the entire document should be considered the worm. W32.Mydoom.AX@mm is an example of a worm.

TIP

Back up your essential data on a regular basis, using a high capacity portable device such as a memory stick. You could also send files to your own e-mail address; a copy will remain on your web server.

How can the use of HTML code save me money?

You can save money by hosting any additional pictures on another website and referencing them from your listing. There are several hosting companies on the internet which will allow you to upload your pictures for free. For example, www.photobucket.com and www.tinypic.com are easy to use and very popular within the eBay community. To find out what other services are currently available, just ask the question on the community discussion boards: "How do I find a free picture hosting company?"

These companies will allocate you an amount of web space for storing pictures. They do not charge for this service, and once loaded onto the site, pictures can be placed inside your eBay listings. I cannot go into great detail about the process of opening an account with every free picture hosting company as there may be dozens that I do not even know about, and each may have a slightly different way of operating. However, once created, the process of loading a picture to their site is exactly the same as that used for the eBay pictures; you just browse your computer for the picture and then upload it.

Let's say you've opted to use Photobucket.com and uploaded a photo. It is now ready to be used in your eBay listing – just one small line of HTML code to copy and paste. Under your picture are three boxes with codes in them. They will look like a foreign language if you have not seen HTML before, but it is not important that you know what they mean at this stage. The middle box is called 'Tag' and it is the contents of this box that need to be copied. It will look something like this:

```
<img src=http://img.photobucket.com/albums/v260/youruserid/
yourpicture.jpg alt="Image hosted by Photobucket.com">
```

Once you have copied the codes, they can be pasted directly into an eBay listing. This is done at the "Titles & Description" stage. This section of the eBay listing is where you will describe your item. This can be done via a standard method or you can "enter your own HTML". If you select the HTML option, you will see your listing in HTML format, which can look very daunting. Trial and error will determine the best place to insert the codes and load in your picture.

What steps can I take to limit the chances of something going wrong?

These are my top five tips:

1 Be suspicious of attachments that arrive on e-mails from unknown sources.

2 Some viruses can send emails and attachments that appear to have been sent by people you know. If in any doubt, confirm with the sender that they did in fact send it.

3 Do not set your e-mail program to 'auto-run' attachments.

4 Keep your computer fully updated with all security releases.

5 Back up all of the important data regularly and keep the back up copies in a safe location.

Chapter 16

Accounts And Tax

Introduction

I'll be honest – I really hate the paperwork. All that effort keeping my accounts in order and updating stock inventories, it's a wonder I make any money at all. It's all about getting the right process in place and then finding the time to keep it all up to date.

Some admin chores are more important than others; you are not likely to end up in jail for overstating your stock levels, but you might just if you don't pay your VAT.

The following section proves that you are not alone; almost all eBay traders have a dislike of admin. There is a definite trend concerning taxation in its many forms; a subject that is close to many a traders' heart.

The distinction between book-keeping and accounting is very important and can really hit your pocket if you get it wrong. With a little thought and a good 'day to day' process in place you should have a better idea of how your business is doing. Quick tip: swap all those receipts from your shoebox into a nice new ring binder – tax deductible of course!

My advice is to read this chapter once, then a second time and then make that call to hire an accountant.

How do I calculate an item's cost for tax purposes?

The good news is that you don't have to have a separate receipt for each item that you sell; it is the overall profit which needs to be calculated. If you buy a large mixed lot and the items are of a similar value, just divide the total cost by the number of items and enter this as the purchase price. If the lot has some more valuable items in it, allocate a higher cost to these and then split the remaining amount amongst the other items. The important thing is that the purchase price is entered along with the sum of the sales so that the overall profit of your eBay business can be calculated.

> I also buy stock which does not have a receipt; I simply record the item, date, location and price paid into a small book. This book is effectively a receipt of each purchase, the total of which is entered each month as a purchases figure.

Do I need to worry about capital gains tax on my trading profits?

Capital gains tax (CGT) is a very complex area. If your items are of significant value, I would advise that you consult an expert before listing them on eBay.

CGT is a tax on the increase in the capital value of an item. You normally only have to pay CGT when you no longer own an asset, that is when you have disposed of it. This is the HM Revenue &

Customs (HMR&C) definition and the ruling applies to most assets that are bought and then sold for a higher value. It is the *difference* between the purchase and sale price that may be liable to tax.

Each individual has a personal allowance, which varies from year to year, and there is also an indexation allowance calculator which is used for assets that were purchased some years ago. As a general rule, only high value items will be considered for capital gains. The HMR&C leaflet at www.hmrc.gov.uk/cgt outlines the circumstances in which it might be paid.

For the year 2007/08 the CGT allowance for an individual is £9,200, with any gain over this amount taxed at your highest marginal rate, hence the reason to seek professional advice. As a general rule, personal goods or 'chattels' are only liable to CGT if they are over £6,000 in value. This includes single items and collections of items which make up a set of some kind; a collection of 6 paintings by the same painter each with a value of £2,000 that were bought for £1,000 each might be liable, whereas a single painting might not.

eBay will not inform HMR&C about any specific trades as the responsibility rests with the individual. They will however provide information if requested to do so.

What is the best system to employ to keep my books?

There are two main ways to keep books for an eBay business; the first is to use a method known as 'cash accounting', the second option is a system based on 'accruals'.

Cash accounting is only concerned with the movement of money; you ignore the date of the sale and instead just monitor payments to and by your business. HMR&C accept this as a valid accounting method and it will remove the need to 'un-sell' something if the buyer doesn't pay. Using cash-based accounting, income and expenses are recognised only when cash is received or paid out.

The accruals method records everything that impacts on the 'net worth' of your business; both debtors and creditors. When an eBay sale takes place, you have a debtor (the buyer) who is likely to pay you within a few days. If you buy your stock on credit from a wholesaler, you become their debtor and they are your creditor. Both of these transactions will alter the net worth of your business.

As accounts are drawn to a close once a year, it is likely that you will be owed some money for sales during the last few days of the year, and you may also have prepaid some bills; these are regarded as assets of the business. At the end of the tax year you will need to work out how many buyers still owe you money. Those who are likely to pay will be recorded as an asset on your balance sheet as debtors, whereas those who you suspect may not pay need to be recorded as 'Bad or doubtful debt'.

I would lean towards an accruals based system as you will be carrying stock for some time. This will make some extra work, but should give a fairer picture of your business position. As always, seek professional advice.

How should I record my business activities on eBay?

When you have been trading for a year, you will need to submit your tax return, which will detail all of your income from eBay and from any other sources you have. If you have kept some simple records during the year, you will only have to copy a few figures into your tax return. HM Revenue & Customs are unlikely to want to see your detailed records, but you never know.

How you record your business activities is really down to personal choice. There are some computer packages available or you could consult an accountant. You could also create your own spreadsheet or just write them down on paper. You must decide how best to do this for you, but once you have settled on a method, keep things up to date on a regular basis and filling in your tax return shouldn't be too bad.

What is the tax position if I buy a job lot of goods, and keep some of the contents but re-sell the rest?

This situation is one that I am familiar with; I often buy whole collections of various items, keep some, sell some and find that some pieces are damaged.

My own experience with the taxman is that common sense usually prevails. I would divide the purchase price by the number of items (including any broken ones), and use this price to set against any profit made from selling them. Broken items, bad buys, etc. can also be written off against profits, so record them somewhere as well.

Items that you buy for your own collection are generally not liable to tax when you sell them, as you didn't buy them with the intention to sell.

There may be capital gains tax if the items are of a high value. How long you keep them before selling may also be a consideration. HM Revenue & Customs has to be realistic with second-hand / collectable items – it is hard to tell for sure how long you have had them.

Do I need to pay National Insurance?

You should register for National Insurance, although you may not need to pay any. These contributions build up your entitlements to various benefits, with perhaps the most important being your state pension. Just to make things more interesting, there are currently 4 types known as Classes 1 to 4. As a self-employed person you will need to register for Class 2, and if you do well, you will need to pay class 4 as well. If you are employed and operate eBay in your spare time, you may well be paying class 1 already.

Here's how it works; Class 2 is required for self-employed people, it is not dependant upon income, just a flat rate payment each week. If your profits are above a certain level (around £5,000 per year) then you will pay a percentage of them as well.

Some good news: If your profits are likely to be low, you can apply for a National Insurance Class 2 exemption certificate. If you are successful with your application, your NI contributions will be paid for you until your business becomes more profitable. This certificate is valid for three years, but can be extended beyond this period if you fill in another form.

As with personal tax liabilities, it may be wise to set aside NI contributions throughout the year as you may well do better than you expected and end up owing more than you think. If your business does not do well, at least you won't get an NI bill through the post. Speak to your local tax office about your personal circumstances.

What trading expenses can I claim for an eBay business?

The true cost of selling in any business will vary; there is the cost of the stock and then the cost of actually selling and running the business. With an eBay business, the costs can be quite varied, although there are some that would apply to almost all areas.

These expenses will reduce the amount of profit you make from your trading activities, so it is important to record them all. It is also important not to inflate them as this may cause problems when you submit your tax return.

Typical expenses will include:

- Packing materials

- Stamps

- Staff wages

- Heat and light

- Insurance

- Fuel costs

- Stationary costs (paper, ink)

- Telephone lines

- Bank charges

- eBay charges

- PayPal charges

- Rent

- Training

In addition to these running costs, your business will also need some equipment before it can trade. The list of items will vary, but is likely to include:

- Computers

- Printers

- Mobile phone

Items of a higher value such as a computer can be depreciated over a period of time. This allowance for replacement can be included as a business expense.

What are the 'current assets' on a balance sheet?

The first thing to point out is that if you are selling on eBay as a sole trader then you need only prepare a profit and loss account, whereas if you are VAT registered or running a very large business you will need a balance sheet as well.

The balance sheet is really just a record of where the money is in a business at a particular point in time (usually the end of a financial year). It shows the value of assets and liabilities and the value of the owner's share.

Assets come in two flavours; fixed (capital) and current. Fixed assets might include buildings, computers or even digital cameras. The value of these assets is recorded at their current book value (after any allowance for depreciation). Current assets include stock that remains unsold (again at its current value), money owed by customers and any prepaid bills.

Current liabilities (the next section) will include money owed to suppliers, unpaid bills and so on.

The third section of a balance sheet shows to whom the assets and liabilities belong, usually the proprietor or shareholders. The entries in this section will 'balance' with the total of the net assets. This section might include profit from previous years that had been reinvested, profit from the current year, and any capital provided to the business.

What should I do if my stock is worth less than I paid for it?

The good news is that you only really need to think about this once a year; when you compile your annual trading figures.

The first thing to complete is a thorough stock take on the last day of your tax year. Make a list of everything you have left and record the value based on the price you paid for the item.

Some of your stock may have no value; it may be damaged or returned goods. This stock also needs to be recorded and given a value based on the price that it was bought for. This figure will be written off from your remaining stock assets.

You may also have stock that is still of some value, but less than the price you originally paid. When you do sell it, it will be at a loss. This stock needs to be written down to an achievable value; again this will impact on your total asset value.

> This assessment of stock value is also necessary in order to determine just how much you sold during the year; the calculation is: opening stock + cost of sales − closing stock. The closing stock figure is then adjusted to take account of written down or written off stock.

How do I work out the profit on my eBay trading?

Book-keeping is my biggest headache. I hate admin. I think most salespeople do. I still use a very simple spreadsheet to record all my trading activities.

> Going legitimate with the taxman is not as bad as you might think. By the time you have factored in all of your operating costs, profit will (sadly) be very scarce indeed.

The basic idea is to first work out your sales figure or turnover. eBay provide help with this in the form of a download file. Next is the amount you spend on stock, and for this I just record each purchase in a book and keep any receipts as a back up.

Sales minus the cost of those sales will equal your gross profit.

Next come the expenses, which can be quite a list; just keep a record of any business costs and transfer them to your spreadsheet each month. Keep another book to record business journeys as these are also a business expense and tax deductible.

Gross profit - expenses = net profit and it is this that you will be taxed on after any allowances.

This is of course a simple overview of how it works, but it should get you started. As activity starts to grow, investigate purpose built systems and always seek professional advice from an accountant.

When should I register my eBay business with the taxman?

Tax is very topical at the moment, as the government seems to think that some people may be trading on eBay and not declaring their income!

You should register your business activities with HM Revenue & Customs within 3 months of starting trading. If this deadline has passed you may be liable to a fine of £100.

The rules are quite simple; anybody who buys with the intention to resell is deemed to be trading and any profits are taxable. PowerSellers and those with large feedback scores are most likely to be doing this, so I guess the taxman will start looking there first.

If you are selling a variety of different used items that you have just acquired over the years, you should be fine as this is not considered as trading for tax purposes. If you sell lots of similar used goods, HMR&C may decide that there is just too much to be from a personal collection and delve further into your account.

The key phrase used by HMR&C is "air of commerciality". If your activities are such that this can be inferred, then you should contact their helpline on 0845 915 4515.

235

You will need to keep detailed records of your purchases, sales and all expenses. Feed these into a spreadsheet or accounting software program and your net profit should emerge.

For purchases without receipts, create your own and file them with the rest and for eBay purchases, keep a copy of your invoice.

Once a year, usually in May or June, HMR&C will send you a self assessment tax form, which you will need to complete with details of your income for the past year. Any net profit from your eBay trading will be added to any other income and taxed in accordance with your personal allowances.

When do I need to register for VAT?

VAT is calculated on turnover (£64,000 2007/08). You should register if you exceed or expect to exceed this level during the year. It is interesting that turnover is deemed to include all 'invoiced monies', that is to say the total amount that you include on your invoice. In the case of an eBay business, this figure includes postage and insurance charges.

You can register for VAT on a voluntary basis with any level of turnover. Think about this carefully beforehand and seek professional advice.

eBay do offer some general advice on this area, however the burden of responsibility rests with the individual trader. For more details contact the HMR&C helpline on 0845 010 9000 (+44 208 929 0152 outside UK).

What are the benefits in voluntarily registering for VAT?

You can register for VAT at any time and it does not depend upon your earnings level; it will be down to a personal choice if it is worth it for you.

Being registered for VAT will involve more paperwork and this must not be overlooked; check the HMR&C website for full details (www.hmrc.gov.uk). Depending on the type of goods you sell and where you source them from, it might be financially advantageous. Currently, the cost of your stock will probably include an element of VAT which will be charged by the supplier; £10.00 of stock will cost you £11.75 if the rate of 17.5% applies, so you will need to sell it at a higher figure than that to make a profit.

If you opt for VAT registration, you will need to include an element of VAT on your invoices (along with your VAT number). This will be at whatever rate is applicable (0%, 5%, and 17.5% are the most common). The VAT paid by your customer is known as the 'output' VAT. You will still continue to pay your suppliers the same amount; this is your 'input' VAT.

When you complete your VAT return, the input VAT is deducted from the output VAT and the difference paid to HMRC. In some circumstances this may result in a refund.

As you must now charge your customer VAT on your sale price, this may impact on your turnover if the item becomes too expensive.

The other point of interest is that many of your business expenses also include an element of VAT. These include stationery, computers, printers, office furniture, heat and lighting, internet connections, telephone calls, eBay fees and so on. It may be that you will be able to claim back some of this VAT.

Seek professional advice from an accountant before deciding either way.

Is it necessary to employ an accountant for my eBay business?

No, but remember that any fees you pay to an accountant will be tax deductible, but of course they will already know that.

There is a difference between 'accounting' and 'book-keeping'; the latter is all about recording the day to day business transactions, filing receipts, updating mileage records and so on, and you certainly would not want to pay an accountant to do this for you. An accountant will be able to use your business details to produce your profit & loss account, balance sheet if required and prepare your tax return. On a more practical level, an accountant will know which expenses can be claimed in connection with your business and this alone may save you enough tax to cover their fees.

As a rule of thumb, the more complex your business becomes, the more I would recommend that you use the services of an accountant.

Do I need to be trading as a limited company if I am running a business on eBay?

No. You do not need to have limited liability; sole trader status is fine, with any eBay profit simply added to your other earnings when you fill in your tax return.

If you make a loss on your eBay activity, this can be offset against any tax paid on other activities, but only in the same tax year.

Conclusion

Congratulations on making it to the end of the book. I hope you enjoyed the journey through the world of eBay question by question and found the answers you were looking for.

I have really enjoyed writing this book and it has been a pleasure to assist other eBay members along the way. I would like to thank everybody who has taken the trouble to write to me over the past year or so, and please accept my apologies if your question didn't make it into this book.

There is no doubt that eBay can produce a source of income and a real alternative to the '9 to 5', however it can also be a great way to meet virtual friends. Through my weekly writings I have made many new friends and learnt so much myself along the way. Here's to the next year on eBay!

We do have space for just one more before we run headlong into the Appendices:

Where can I go to get more help with my eBay activities?

This is an easy question; sign up for my free weekly newsletter "The eBay UK Bulletin" at www.ebaybulletin.co.uk.

Each week I receive e-mails concerning all aspects of eBay life; the clean ones will be published either in the bulletin or on the website. Check it out from time to time as new thoughts, stories, tips and comments are being posted every day.

Appendices

Glossary of terms and abbreviations

Throughout eBay many abbreviations are used to save time and space, particularly in the restricted title box. This list is by no means complete but, it contains the common terms and the ones I feel are more pertinent to selling.

BIN
Buy It Now

BNWT
Brand New With Tag

Browse
How to find general items.

Dutch Auction
Used when offering multiple items that are identical for sale. Multiple item auctions can have many winners, all of which pay the same price, which is the lowest successful bid.

FVF
Final Value Fee

Gallery
The small picture which can sit alongside the item title in the search results page.

HTML
Hypertext Markup Language

ISP

Internet Service Provider

Inventory

The stock you have for sale or awaiting sale.

JPG

Pronounced 'J-Peg', this is a file format for images.

Keyword spamming

Using top search words within your auction to attract visitors but which do not relate to any aspect of your auction.

Link

Text or a picture that sits on a web page, usually the description or "About Me" page, that if clicked will take you to another page of the internet. Also known as a 'hyperlink'.

MIB

Mint In Box

Mint

The item is in perfect condition.

MIP

Mint in Packet

MOC

Mint on Card

NARU

Not A Registered User. A suspended account.

NR

No Reserve

NPB

Non-Paying Bidder

Newbie

Somebody who is new to eBay.

OOP

Out of Print or Production

PayPal

An eBay company, allowing buyers and sellers to send and receive money via an electronic medium.

Reserve

The price below which the item will not sell even if it has bids.

ROI

Return on Investment

SYI

Sell Your Item. Usually refers to the form.

Search

How to find specific items.

Second Chance Offer

A feature of all standard auction listings that will allow you to make offers to any under-bidders at their highest bid price.

Sig

Signature

Spam

Unwanted emails often offering items for sale without the receiver's consent.

URL

Uniform Resource Locator. The address for a web page.

VHTF

Very Hard To Find

Vintage

Goods produced before 1980.

Prohibited items

The items below are prohibited for sale on eBay.

Aeroplane Tickets	Lock-picking Devices
Alcohol	Lottery Tickets
Animals and wildlife products	Mailing Lists and Personal Information
Catalogue and URL Sales	Multi-level Marketing, Pyramid, Matrix and Trading Schemes
Counterfeit Currency and Stamps	
Counterfeit and Trademarked Items	Offensive Material
Credit Cards	Prescription Drugs and Materials
Drugs and Drug paraphernalia	Recalled Items
Embargoed Items & Prohibited Countries	Satellite, Digital and Cable TV Decoders
	Shares and Securities
Firearms and Ammunition	Stolen Items
Fireworks	Surveillance Equipment
Franking Machines	Tobacco and Tobacco Products
Football Tickets	Train Tickets
Government IDs, Licences and Uniforms	Travel Vouchers
Human Parts and Remains	Unlocking Software

Questionable items

Adults Only	Pesticides
Artefacts	Plants and Seeds
Autographed Items	Police-Related Items
Batteries	Pre-sales Listings
British Titles	Slot Machines
CFC and HCFC Refrigerants	Used Clothing
Contracts and Tickets	Used Medical Devices
Electronics Equipment	Weapons & Knives
Food	
Hazardous, Restricted and Perishable Items	

Index

Chapter 1 Registration And ID

Chapter 2 Buying Issues

Chapter 3 Deciding What To Sell

Chapter 4 Sourcing Products To Sell

Chapter 5 Listing Items For Sale

Chapter 6 Mechanics Of The Sale

Chapter 7 Postage And Delivery

Chapter 8 Packing

Chapter 9 When Transactions Go Wrong

Chapter 10 Feedback

Chapter 11 Payment

Chapter 12 Fees, Duties And Charges

Chapter 13 Scams

Chapter 14 Trading For A Living

Chapter 15 Technology

Chapter 16 Accounts And Tax

Conclusion